The Future of JavaScript

Coding Interactive Websites: A Beginner's Guide to JavaScript

Olivia Davis

Table of Contents

INTRODUCTION

JavaScript is the main engine of the contemporary web development process. JavaScript still runs the most dynamic, responsive, and interactive websites we use on a regular basis, even if the digital world is always changing. JavaScript is the invisible force that helps everything run effortlessly; examples of this are real time updates on news platforms, flawless social media feed performance, and flawless e-commerce checkout functionality. The Future of JavaScript - Coding Interactive Websites: A Beginner's Guide to JavaScript is meant to help you, the beginning, in taking first confident steps into this dynamic programming language and realizing the possibilities it holds for molding the web of the future.

It is assumed the reader is not familiar with JavaScript or programming previously. First of all, a basic overview of JavaScript's purposes in web development is given. The Future of JavaScript - Coding Interactive Websites is a discussion of how it interacts with HTML and CSS, as well as the reasons interactive web experiences must evolve. By means of this course, you will acquire the skills required to create your development tools, write your first scripts, and notice the instantaneous effects JavaScript may have on a webpage.

As you work through The Future of JavaScript - Coding Interactive Websites, you will get to know basic programming concepts, including variables, data types, loops, functions, and objects. These building elements will help one to understand how logic and interactivity are created in JavaScript. Apart from this, you will get competent in handling the Document Object Model (DOM), which is a necessary competence that helps you to respond to user activities, control and change the content of a webpage in a dynamic way, and build interesting interfaces.

The Future of JavaScript - Coding Interactive Websites emphasizes learning by practical experience. Through means of examples, exercises, and a project appropriate for beginners—the building of an interactive quiz application entirely functioning—your skills will be tested throughout the book. Not only will finishing this project give you an actual result you can also be happy with, but it will also help you better understand JavaScript's structure, event handling, user interaction, and several other subjects.

In terms of the narrative, the last chapter turns the emphasis to the future. JavaScript has developed into a vital part of full-stack development rather than only a programming language grounded on browsers. You will get an overview of strong modern features, including ES6+ syntax, arrow functions, destructuring, and modules.

The Future of JavaScript - Coding Interactive Websites is meant to stimulate your curiosity and provide a strong foundation for your future employment as a software developer, not only to teach syntax. By the time you finish this journey, you will not only know how JavaScript works but also be ready to apply it to realize your ideas, help the current web, and keep your education in an always changing area.

With The Future of JavaScript acting as your portal, both knowing the present and embracing the future of interactive web development is achievable. Let's begin this fascinating trip!

CHAPTER I

Introduction to JavaScript and the Web

The Role of JavaScript in Web Development

For many years, JavaScript has been among the fundamental building blocks of contemporary web development. JavaScript is absolutely essential for consumers' experience of the internet nowadays since it is the language that gives webpages interactivity and behavior. JavaScript is behind a wide range of dynamic capabilities from the moment a web page loads in a browser to the split-second response of a button click. From a basic scripting language to a strong ecosystem supporting client-side and server-side applications, JavaScript's development reflects the increasing complexity and interactivity expected by both modern consumers and companies alike.

JavaScript originated in the early days of the web when digital terrain was dominated by still HTML pages. Originally developed in just ten days by Brendan Eich in

1995, JavaScript was designed to allow dynamic interactions inside web browsers, therefore offering a lightweight alternative to HTML's structure and CSS styling. JavaScript soon acquired popularity despite first being written off by some as a toy language because of its simplicity and instant effect on the user experience. It lets creators add modest animations, content changes, and form validation without having to reload a page—capabilities that transform user expectations and design paradigms.

The demand for more sophisticated client-side behavior developed as websites changed from static documents to dynamic apps. JavaScript was developed with these expectations. Improvements in browser engines and language standards, including ECMAScript standardized JavaScript's syntax and capabilities over the years, guarantee consistent behavior across many settings. JavaScript's global language of the web—a function it still serves today—was made possible by this standardizing. AJAX (Asynchronous JavaScript and XML) allowed JavaScript-enabled websites to obtain data from servers without refreshing the entire page, therefore signifying a big change toward asynchronous communication and real time content changes. By abstraction much of the low-level complexity of DOM manipulation and event handling, these frameworks and libraries enable developers to create highly scalable, maintainable, and performable applications. JavaScript is the language behind all these systems; it powers their components, interactions, and logic.

JavaScript's impact beyond the browser as well. With Node.js's release in 2009, JavaScript's reach to the server side was greatly expanded, and a major turning point was reached. Built on Chrome's V8 JavaScript engine, Node.js lets developers create single programming language full-stack apps. Simplified the learning curve for new developers, increased productivity, and promoted code reuse by means of this front-end and back-end development process unity. JavaScript thus evolved into a very complete-stack language supporting RESTful APIs, WebSocket real time communication, and even file system access.

Through the Node Package Manager (npm), Node.js also spawned a vast ecosystem of packages and modules. From database management to authentication and file processing, developers suddenly have access to reusable solutions for nearly any problem imagined, thanks to millions of packages accessible. Thanks to fast prototyping and less need to reinvent the wheel, this ecosystem has grown to be among the most potent features of JavaScript development. The active community surrounding JavaScript and its tools guarantees that the language keeps changing quickly to meet fresh problems and possibilities as they present.

Apart from Node.js, JavaScript's importance in web development grew with the release of complete-stack JavaScript frameworks such as Meteor, Next.js, and Nuxt.js. These systems let front-end and back-end components be seamlessly integrated, server-side rendering possible, static site generation enabled, and more. They show a rising need for fast load times, enhanced SEO, and responsive user experience high-performance web applications provide. JavaScript's adaptability helps it to be used for everything from basic websites to sophisticated enterprise-level systems, hence reinforcing its general-purpose development language character.

The creation and administration of APIs also depend critically on JavaScript. Modern web apps that must interact with databases, outside-of-server third-party services, and mobile apps depend on REST and GraphQL APIs—often created using JavaScript on the server side. JavaScript tools like Express.js and Apollo Server let developers quickly build paths, manage middleware, handle requests, and effectively serve data. These technologies make JavaScript the perfect choice for creating strong back-ends that effortlessly enable complicated front-end experiences.

Particularly because of frameworks like React, component-based architecture—one of the most radical changes in JavaScript's recent past—is becoming rather common. In self-contained modules that can be reused and assembled to create sophisticated UIs, components capture both logic and presentation in small bits. Reusability, testability, and code readability all get better from this modularity in a world where maintainability and scalability rule, component-driven programming fits exactly the objectives of contemporary online projects. Originally thought of as just a scripting language for little online improvements, JavaScript is today the foundation of increasingly complex and powerful application architectures competing with conventional desktop software.

Integration of JavaScript with browser APIs also enables developers to access device capabilities and enhance user experiences. By means of APIs for geolocation, local storage, drag-and-drop, camera access, and offline capabilities via service workers, developers may create web apps that seem natural on the device they run on. Powered by JavaScript, these Progressive Web Apps (PWAs) blur the boundaries between websites and mobile apps, including offline capability, home screen installation, and push notifications. PWAs help especially in areas with erratic internet access or where app store access is restricted, therefore extending the reach and influence of web-based solutions.

With tools like Jest, Mocha, and Cypress offering complete testing frameworks, JavaScript has also found its way into the field of testing and automation. A key component of software development, automated testing guarantees dependability and scale-based performance. Within the same environment as the program itself, JavaScript lets developers create end-to-end integration and unit tests. This consistency lowers context switching and streamlines the pipeline of continuous integration and deployment (CI/CD), hence improving general output.

JavaScript excels in real time communication as well. For uses including live chat, multiplayer gaming, and collaborative products like Google Docs, technologies like WebSockets—which let a client and a server engage in bi-directional communication—have changed everything. By abstracting the complexity of real time data flow, JavaScript frameworks like Socket.IO let developers create highly interactive and responsive apps that quickly change depending on user behavior or system events. In the web of today, where users demand instant response and interaction, this capacity is absolutely necessary.

One cannot stress the part JavaScript plays in improving user experience. Early days saw frameworks like jQuery provide developers easy access to DOM manipulation, animations, and event handling. Every modern JavaScript application feed on the idea of enhancing the interactivity and responsiveness of web pages, even if modern frameworks have essentially supplanted jQuery. JavaScript lets you create responsive interfaces, dynamic loading, seamless transitions, and contextual user feedback. Without it, the web would still be a fixed collection of hyperlinked texts rather than the rich, immersive ecosystems consumers interact with now.

Modern web development now centers on accessibility as well, and JavaScript is essential in creating inclusive experiences. From dynamically changing ARIA characteristics for screen readers to controlling keyboard navigation, developers utilize JavaScript to guarantee that all users—including those with disabilities—may use their applications. Although JavaScript can occasionally create obstacles to access if abused, it also offers the means to remove those obstacles when used deliberately and in line with the best standards. Adaptive layouts and responsive design also depend critically on JavaScript. These elements enable users on a PC, tablet, or mobile phone to access a website seamlessly, therefore increasing engagement and pleasure.

Another vital area where JavaScript has benefits and obligations is security. Against weaknesses such as cross-site scripting (XSS), cross-site request forgery (CSRF), and other client-side exploits, web developers have to be alert. Security best practices are included in modern JavaScript frameworks, and strict mode and Content Security Policy (CSP) tools help to reduce hazards. Usually working in concert with APIs, cookies, and tokens to protect user data and application integrity, JavaScript also actively implements authentication and authorization procedures.

At last, JavaScript's instructional value merits discussion. Aspiring developers would find it the perfect first language because of its somewhat low barrier to entry and instantaneous feedback in the browsers. The learning process is interesting and easily accessible since a basic script included in an HTML file can show obvious results in seconds. Countless courses, boot camps, and online resources devoted to JavaScript help to inspire a fresh generation of developers who will define the web going forward. The changing syntax and features of JavaScript have also been rather important for its staying strength and rising acceptance. These improvements have made JavaScript not only more pleasant to write but also more suited to manage challenging programming concepts, including modular design and asynchronous operations.

Among JavaScript's most potent and difficult features is its asynchronous character. Many times, depending on resources like APIs, databases, and outside services—all of which add latency—web apps rely on JavaScript's event loop and asynchronous handling—through callbacks, promises, and async/await—let developers create non-blocking code that responds to user input and other events continuously while waiting for outside processes to finish. Creating seamless, performable programs that don't stop or turn unresponsive during long-running chores depends on this ability.

Furthermore, TypeScript—a superset of JavaScript with static typing—has addressed one of the most often voiced complaints about JavaScript: its dynamic and rather lazy character. TypeScript increases dependability and maintainability by letting creators find mistakes during compilation instead of running through. Particularly in major projects, it also promotes improved tools, autocompletion, and refactoring. The rising popularity of TypeScript has attracted numerous business-level teams and initiatives into the JavaScript ecosystem, so reinforcing its importance in web development.

Beyond websites and applications, JavaScript is now a pillar of the creation of cross-platform experiences. React Native and Electron, respectively, create native mobile apps and desktop software using JavaScript. While Electron powers desktop apps, including Visual Studio Code and Slack, React Native lets developers create a single JavaScript codebase running on both iOS and Android. By greatly improving speed and consistency across several environments, this cross-platform capability helps teams to provide consistent experiences without keeping separate code bases for every platform. Tightly coupled with JavaScript frameworks and libraries, modern build tools enable continuous integration and delivery pipelines automatically testing, building, and deploying apps. These techniques enhance agile development approaches, cut release cycles, and enable developers to react fast to security concerns or user comments.

JavaScript also facilitates the building of serverless architectures and headless CMS platforms, which have been rather popular in contemporary web development. Headless CMSs like Strapi or Contentful and serverless services from providers like AWS Lambda or Vercel let developers separate the front-end from the back-end and run apps as a suite of functions and APIs. Thanks to its asynchronous character and fit with contemporary cloud architecture, JavaScript is usually the language of choice for these serverless tasks.

The fact that JavaScript shapes the emergence of single-page applications (SPAs) adds still another essential component of its importance in web development. SPAs dynamically refresh the content inside a single page, unlike conventional multi-page applications that reload the whole page upon switching to a new URL. Since only the required bits of the page are re-rendered instead of refreshing the whole page, this method improves user experience by smoothing out interactions and accelerating speed. JavaScript manages the logic underlying routing, state management, and rendering views without requiring complete page reloads; hence, it is at the core of SPAs, along with frameworks like Angular, React, and Vue.js. Modern web expectations have been greatly shaped by the rise of SPAs since consumers now expect quick and flexible browsing environments.

Moreover, real time apps handling live updates depend on JavaScript extensively in development. This covers all from live data dashboards to social media sites. Technologies like Firebase, GraphQL subscriptions, or JavaScript, in conjunction with WebSockets, let developers create apps that update in real time without having the user reload the page. Applications depending on live data, including stock market updates, sports scores, or social media feeds, depend on this capability. It enables companies to give consumers dynamic content, which is vital at a time when consumers demand continual, up-to-date information.

Within the realm of e-commerce, JavaScript keeps redefining the purchasing experience. Progressive web apps (PWAs) enable stores to offer app-like experiences on the web. JavaScript drives offline capabilities, push alerts, and rapid loading speeds, among other things. Since PWAs close the gap between mobile apps and conventional websites so users may access the content they want even when they are offline or with limited network conditions, they have shown to be rather successful in enhancing consumer engagement. JavaScript has changed how merchants and e-commerce companies interact with consumers and present their goods and services.

JavaScript's capacity to be always changing and adaptable is one of the main reasons it keeps flourishing in web development. From a basic tool for adding interaction to websites, the language has evolved dramatically from its beginnings in 1995 to become the potent and sophisticated instrument it is today. New tools, libraries, and frameworks added to JavaScript's ecosystem—all meant to meet the ever more complicated needs of contemporary web development—have surged. The language has stayed fundamentally simple and flexible throughout development, which has made it approachable to novice and experienced programmers alike. Its success can be mostly attributed to this versatility since it lets developers try several tools and techniques free from feeling bound into a specific style of working.

Besides, JavaScript is essential for the democratization of web programming. While more experienced coders may resort to sites like GitHub, Stack Overflow, and community forums to keep current with the newest trends, platforms like Codecademy, freeCode Camp, and MDN Web Docs offer complete resources for novices.

Furthermore, indispensable in contemporary web development is JavaScript's scalability capability. The need for strong, maintainable, and scalable code is more important as websites and applications get more complicated. React, Vue.js, and Angular JavaScript frameworks let developers organize their apps such that scalability is promoted. These models simplify application scaling in terms of features and performance by offering tools for managing application state, efficiently handling big data sets, and grouping code into reusable components. Particularly in the context of component-based architectures, JavaScript's modularity and reusability guarantee that programs remain manageable even as they get in scope and complexity.

JavaScript's quick development also reflects the web's larger movement toward an interactive and immersive user experience. The expectations of users have grown more complex as web apps have developed. Dynamic, interesting experiences and static web pages are bridged in great part by JavaScript. These days, developers may produce interactive components, including interactive forms, real time chat interfaces, sophisticated animations, and even virtual or augmented reality apps. Driven by JavaScript, the depth of these experiences has turned websites from being content delivery platforms into completely dynamic, personalized worlds that instantly react to user actions and preferences.

Libraries like TensorFlow.js have let developers directly include machine learning models straight into their JavaScript code, therefore enabling web applications to handle and analyze client-side data without depending on strong server-side resources. Real time image recognition, voice interaction, recommendation systems, and more are just a few of the many fresh opportunities this skill creates. JavaScript has reduced the barrier to entrance for including artificial intelligence into online apps by enabling machine learning in the browser, therefore allowing developers to experiment with AI models and integrate them into their applications in ways that were formerly difficult and resource-intensive.

Another transforming feature of mobile programming has been the integration of JavaScript. React Native and other frameworks let developers construct a shared codebase, therefore transcending JavaScript's reach outside the desktop and browser. Because developers no longer must create distinct code for every platform, this cross-platform development paradigm not only saves time but also lowers expenses. A major reason JavaScript is so widely used in mobile app development is its capacity to target several platforms with a single codebase; this helps JavaScript to be a necessary tool for creating modern, cross-device applications that effortlessly run across several devices and operating systems.

Apart from its importance in web development, JavaScript has been rather influential in the field of server-side programming. JavaScript was first mostly connected historically with client-side scripting, running in the browser. Back-end development has been transformed, though, with the release of Node.js, a runtime enabling server JavaScript running. Using the same V8 JavaScript engine—the same engine that drives Google Chrome—Node.js offers developers a non-blocking, event-driven architecture fit for managing I/O-heavy applications. This has made it possible for developers to use JavaScript for server-side as well as client-side development, therefore facilitating a more consistent and simplified working environment. Popular frameworks for creating modern online apps, the MEAN stack (MongoDB, Express.js, Angular, Node.js) and MERN stack (MongoDB, Express.js, React, Node.js) have been born out of the full-stack

JavaScript development methodology, which has also resulted in more efficient development processes.

Moreover, JavaScript's application in the creation of APIs has significantly raised its importance in contemporary web development. JavaScript is increasingly used to build RESTful APIs or GraphQL APIs that let several apps or services interact with one another as APIs take the front stage in the architecture of contemporary applications. JavaScript especially fits the development of APIs that can connect with external services, databases, or microservices since it can manage asynchronous activities and make HTTP queries. Building these APIs helps developers create sophisticated systems that combine data and capabilities from many sources, therefore giving consumers a more dynamic and customized experience.

While progressively adding sophisticated features—often driven by JavaScript—that improve the user experience in newer browsers, progressive enhancement lets developers create a baseline. This guarantees that, regardless of their surroundings, every user has access to a functional online experience; those with more contemporary technology can benefit from the additional capabilities. JavaScript has been a major force in the field of web development thanks in great part to this inclusive and accessible attitude.

JavaScript stays essential on the technological stack as web development develops. JavaScript has constantly changed to fit the evolving needs of the web, from the early days of adding simple interactivity to websites to its present position as the basis of sophisticated, data-driven web applications. Modern web developers use the language since its adaptability and rich ecosystem of libraries, frameworks, and tools reflect their own choices. JavaScript will remain a pillar of web development for years to come because of its ability to enable rich user experiences, support server-side apps, enable mobile and desktop development, and mix modern technologies, including machine learning.

One of the most amazing patterns as JavaScript develops is its increasing participation in Internet of Things (IoT) applications. The IoT revolution has given developers fresh difficulties since it links regular appliances to the internet for data sharing and communication. The interaction and management of these devices are being made possible in great part by JavaScript. Built on Node.js, libraries such as Johnny-Five let developers use JavaScript to control hardware, including sensors, motors, and lights. This has helped to open the path for home automation systems and smart devices. JavaScript is a top contender for running IoT apps because of its simplicity, adaptability, and compatibility with other tools, therefore extending the reach of web development well beyond conventional desktop and mobile applications.

Still another area of major influence is JavaScript's inclusion into the realm of cloud computing. JavaScript has become a major factor in the evolution of cloud-native apps as cloud-based platforms like AWS, Google Cloud, and Microsoft Azure proliferate. These systems let developers create scalable and robust apps; JavaScript is frequently used via APIs and serverless architectures to communicate with cloud services. While JavaScript makes it simpler to work with these platforms because of its asynchronous character and capacity to smoothly connect with cloud services, serverless computing lets developers concentrate on developing code free from infrastructure management concerns. JavaScript's adaptability guarantees it stays relevant in this environment as cloud computing becomes more and more important, enabling developers to produce scalable and reasonably priced apps.

JavaScript's adaptability for several databases is among its main benefits. Although languages like SQL have long been used in database management, the emergence of NoSQL databases like MongoDB has underlined JavaScript's vital part in data storage and control. Working with NoSQL databases is ideal for JavaScript since it stores data in JSON-like forms, which fits naturally for data management and manipulation. For full-stack web development, especially in the MEAN and MERN stacks, MongoDB is extensively utilized in concert with JavaScript. JavaScript's position as a complete front-end and back-end development solution is even more reinforced by this synergy between JavaScript and NoSQL databases.

Additionally helping JavaScript's endurance and appeal in web development is its support of functional programming paradigms. Emphasizing immutability, higher-order functions, and declarative code, functional programming—which stresses—has become popular in the JavaScript community.

JavaScript is even more useful given the rising market for cross-platform development. Developers are not limited in their building to one platform or device type anymore. JavaScript has spread into desktop application development using frameworks like Electron. Electron lets developers create cross-platform desktop apps with web technologies, allowing JavaScript code to execute effortlessly across Linux, macOS, and Windows, among other operating systems. This change has expanded JavaScript's use outside the web by enabling developers to use known web-based development tools and construct fully functional desktop programs that fit nicely with the underlying operating system.

Progressive Web Apps (PWAs) are another key capability of JavaScript. Acting as mobile apps, PWAs are websites with offline capabilities, push notifications, and quick loading times. The technology enabling PWAs is JavaScript in concert with service workers. Even in the lack of an internet connection, apart from the main browser thread, able to cache material, synchronize data, and complete other chores, improving the user experience. This creative approach to web development has produced applications that may be installed straight on a user's device, therefore offering a native app-like experience free from the necessity of an app store. The way developers see creating apps for the web and mobile devices has changed with JavaScript's support of PWAs.

Growing dependence on JavaScript has also resulted in the creation of complex developer tools that improve the web building process. JavaScript is supported natively in integrated development environments (IDEs), including Visual Studio Code, Sublime Text, and WebStorm, providing potent tools including version control integration, syntactic highlighting, and debugging. Tools for browser developers have also made debugging JavaScript code more straightforward. By means of real time analysis of JavaScript code execution in the browser, these tools help developers spot performance bottlenecks, correct bugs, and improve their code for maximum efficiency. As web applications become increasingly complicated, developers must create dependable, efficient, and maintainable JavaScript code using these potent tools.

The community of JavaScript has been rather important in its development and general acceptance. The community has created a rich ecosystem of open-source libraries, frameworks, and tools that enable developers to learn and grow with JavaScript more readily. By allowing developers to share their work and cooperate on projects, sites like GitHub and npm have helped to create an always growing toolkit of tools to hasten their processes.

JavaScript is not without difficulties, notwithstanding all its developments. JavaScript's uneven behavior across several browsers and devices is one of its continuous problems. There are still differences, even if contemporary browsers have made great progress in standardized JavaScript execution. JavaScript will surely change to fit the needs of the always shifting web development scene as new technologies arrive and user expectations keep rising. JavaScript has a bright future since it keeps influencing how creators of interactive, interesting, and creative online applications build their works.

One of the most important changes in JavaScript's terrain as it develops is its interaction with newly invented technologies. Adoption of it in the field of artificial intelligence (AI) and machine learning (ML) is one instance. Although languages like Python and JavaScript are now also employed in this field, historically, AI and ML were dominated by languages. Using JavaScript, libraries like TensorFlow.js let developers create and test machine learning models straight in the browser. For web apps, this creates fresh opportunities like artificial intelligence-driven features free from server-side processing and real time predictions. To improve interaction and user experience, developers might now include sentiment analysis tools, language translation, or facial recognition capabilities into websites. JavaScript is positioned as a major participant in the future of intelligent online apps thanks to its adaptability together with AI and ML features.

JavaScript and tools like A-Frame and Three.js let developers create immersive AR and VR experiences straight in the browser. Without having to install heavy software or apps, these JavaScript-powered AR/VR applications let users interact with 3D models, explore virtual worlds, and experience interactive media. JavaScript is leading this change and offers a link between the conventional web and innovative immersive technologies since it allows one to create AR/VR experiences in the browser, therefore making these technologies more accessible and user-friendly.

Blockchain and distributed apps (dApps) have also found JavaScript's way into their scene. JavaScript has proven to be a necessary language for creating distributed apps as blockchain technology keeps upsetting sectors by providing a safe, decentralized method of storing and passing data. Using JavaScript, libraries like Web3.js help developers interface with Ethereum and other blockchain networks, thereby creating smart contracts, bitcoin wallets, and distributed finance (DeFi) systems. JavaScript is likely to be a key instrument in the creation of distributed apps as blockchain technology expands, therefore helping to propel the distributed web, sometimes known as Web 3.0.

Apart from these creative advancements, JavaScript's part in accessibility is growingly crucial. Web accessibility guarantees that persons with different disabilities—including those of blindness, deafness, or motor limitations—may use websites and applications. JavaScript's accessibility features are essential in making sure that every user, regardless of their ability, may have a flawless and fair experience as the web grows more inclusive.

JavaScript has been crucial in the change that single-page applications (SPAs) bring about in how developers approach web development. The need for code optimization and speed improvement becomes more important as online applications get ever more complicated. From high-powered desktop computers to mobile phones with limited resources, JavaScript developers have to always concentrate on improving their code to guarantee that it performs effectively across all devices. Another approach to improve speed for demanding apps is the release of WebAssembly (Wasm), which lets developers run code created in languages including C, C++, or Rust alongside JavaScript. JavaScript's flexibility and fit with these new technologies guarantee that it will always be a major factor in web development optimization.

Using these open-source libraries, frameworks, and tools will help developers avoid re-engineering the wheel and concentrate on creating distinctive, creative features. By use of community-driven resources, JavaScript developers may rapidly adopt new trends and best practices, therefore maintaining the language agile and flexible as the web develops.

Furthermore, progressive and creative front-end technologies have developed thanks in great part to JavaScript. JavaScript has been especially important in making sure websites run perfectly across a variety of devices and screen sizes as responsive web design has emerged. JavaScript frameworks include Bootstrap and Foundation as well as CSS libraries let developers construct adaptable and flexible web designs. Using these technologies helps developers guarantee that their online apps provide a consistent user experience. Since JavaScript lets websites reach a larger audience and offer a better user experience, its importance in responsive design has grown to be indispensable for contemporary web development.

At last, JavaScript's future in web development appears to be very bright. JavaScript will always be at the center of these developments as web technologies change, running interactive webpages, mobile apps, IoT devices, artificial intelligence and machine learning applications, blockchain systems, and more. JavaScript's adaptability, community support, and ongoing development guarantee that it will be a necessary tool for web developers for years to come. JavaScript will keep changing and giving developers the tools they need to head-on as the need for more complex, dynamic, and immersive web experiences rises. JavaScript will surely remain a pillar of modern web development for the foreseeable future given its ever-expanding importance in the development of web apps and developing technologies.

Setting Up Your Development Environment

Creating a development environment is among the first and most important actions towards successful programming. Whether your work is on web development, software engineering, or mobile apps, the best performance depends on a consistent, efficient, customized environment. All the tools and technologies a developer needs to write, test, and implement their code fall within the development environment. Every element contributes in different ways to guarantee the code is clean, error-free, and optimized for its intended application and to aid in simplifying the development process.

Selecting the appropriate hardware and operating system comes first in creating a development environment. Enough processing capability, memory, and storage on your computer should enable it to meet the rigors of your development activity. Although macOS's Unix-based system and elegant interface appeal to some developers, others might select Windows or Linux depending on project needs or personal inclination. Because macOS fits Apple's development tools—like Xcode—it is especially well-liked for iOS and macOS app creation. Conversely, Linux is sometimes preferred for server-side development because of its dependability and open-source character. Though historically not as developer-friendly, Windows has made great progress recently, especially with the launch of Windows Subsystem for Linux (WSL), which lets developers run Linux-based tools and utilities straight on Windows.

The process of creating your first JavaScript program could turn out to be an exciting and satisfying experience mixed with uncertainty. JavaScript is generally considered one of the most often used and flexible programming languages available worldwide; it allows a great spectrum of applications to be produced. Among these apps are those related to server-side programming, mobile app production, and even interactive website building. If you want to be a competent programmer, you must understand how to create even the most basic of projects. Learning how to create programs is the first step you should take if you wish to become a skilled programmer, as there is a language that is very important in the evolution of present websites. Starting with writing and running your first JavaScript program will help you to have a basic knowledge of how the JavaScript programming language functions and how browsers interpret JavaScript.

Starting from here requires a basic awareness of the surroundings in which JavaScript runs. Unlike many other programming languages, JavaScript is used somewhat widely in web browsers to create dynamic websites. This is a notable difference whether one compares the performance of these languages in stand-alone programs or development environments. Once you get to this stage, downloading any specific tool or program will not be required for you to begin coding JavaScript. All that is needed to finish this procedure is a web browser and a text editor—two things most personal computers often provide. The medium via which HTML and CSS components that define the structure and style of a webpage interact is JavaScript, a programming language run within the browser. Because of its seamless integration, which helps developers build interactive features, validate forms, and dynamically update content, JavaScript is a basic tool for frontend development.

Starting the process of creating your first JavaScript application is customary to start with a basic script first stage. Fundamentally, a JavaScript script is a piece of code that might be included in an HTML document. Sometimes, people call them scripts. A page loads and the code tells the browser what actions it should take. Most of the time, these behaviors involve changing the displayed content or reacting to user inputs such as clicking, mouse movement, or keyboard entry of text. The most basic type of JavaScript application that one can create is one that just lets the browser show a message. Usually, the way one achieves this is by using the alert feature. Starting here shows how JavaScript can interact with the user by displaying a pop-up message on the screen. Starting this is a fantastic approach. It also introduces the idea of functions, which are basically tiny bits of code meant to do certain operations and may be reused.

Installing the required software tools is quite vital once the operating system has been selected. Usually foremost among these tools is a text editor or IDE. While IDEs come with many more features, text editors are lightweight and offer basic capability for creating code. Among the most often used text editors are Atom, Visual Studio Code, and Sublime Text. Developers of all stripes will find these free, lightweight, and simple to set up editors. Visual Studio Code (VS Code) has been somewhat well-known recently because of its extensive spectrum of extensions, support of several programming languages, and comprehensive debugging features. Conversely, IDEs such as IntelliJ IDEA, Eclipse, and PyCharm offer developers working in certain languages, including Java, Python, or Kotlin, a complete solution. Although IDEs are bulkier than text editors, they offer a more feature-rich development experience, including built-in tools for testing, compiling, and running code.

Establishing the programming languages and frameworks you intend to use for your development initiatives comes next. The language will affect the way these utilities are installed. To create a Python development environment, for instance, download the most recent version from the official Python website and install extra libraries using the pip package manager. Conversely, JavaScript developers might install Node.js, which comprises the npm package manager to manage libraries and dependencies required for JavaScript development. Depending on your framework, web development typically requires installing extra tools such as web browsers, JavaScript engines, and front-end frameworks like React, Angular, or Vue.js. Along with server-side frameworks like Express.js or Django, back-end development could call for database management systems like MySQL, PostSQL, or MongoDB to handle data storage and retrieval.

Still, another essential element of a development environment is version control systems. By far the most often used version control system is Git, which also is a necessary tool for handling code modifications across time. Git lets programmers monitor changes in their codebase, work with other developers, and keep several iterations of their projects. Platforms, including GitHub, GitLab, and Bitbucket link with Git to offer repository hosting, therefore facilitating code sharing and teamwork among other developers. Install the Git program on your computer and set your username and email address for commit-able changes. Git can be accessed straight through the command line or using GUI applications such as SourceTree or GitHub Desktop. A pillar of every development environment, using Git for version control guarantees that developers may roll back to prior versions of their code, track problems, and properly work with others.

It's crucial to set up the surroundings for testing and debugging once the main development tools are set up. Ensuring that your code runs as expected and that it does not bring mistakes depends on testing frameworks, including Jest, Mocha, or JUnit. Developers create unit tests, integration tests, and functional tests—all distinct kinds of tests used to ensure that their code runs as intended. A solid testing environment guarantees that before it is put into use in production, any code you create can be verified for performance and correctness. Examining and fixing code also depends critically on built-in debugging tools in IDEs like Chrome DevTools for JavaScript programmers. These tools let you rapidly identify and fix problems by letting you establish breakpoints, walk through your code, and run through variable inspections at runtime. Simulators or emulators could be used for mobile development to test apps in settings that replicate actual use.

Ensuring your development environment can manage deployment and automated chores becomes more important as the complexity of your project rises. Jenkins, CircleCI, or GitHub Actions are Continuous Integration/Continuous Deployment (CI/CD) systems that assist in automating code development, testing, and deployment. Including these technologies in your development process will help you to guarantee that your application is always deployable, performing automated tests every time you modify something. All of this support a better development experience, these tools can also aid with automating repetitive chores, including linting code, running unit tests, and deploying to production. Applications can also be contained using Docker, therefore offering a consistent development environment independent of the computer you are working on. Developers may package their apps along with all the dependencies they require using Docker so that they work on any system in the same manner.

Establishing a suitable development environment also entails configuring storage systems and databases. Your application may call for non-relational databases like

MongoDB or Redis or relational databases like MySQL or Postgresion installed and configured. Effective storing and retrieving data depend on these databases. Usually involving software installation, database creation, and codebase connection string configuration, database set up is Configuring a local server environment is quite common for web applications. For PHP-based projects, this can entail configuring XAMPP or MAMP, or Node.js with Express.js for JavaScript-based apps. You should also give the security of the tools and frameworks you apply top priority when setting the development environment. To guard against typical threats, including SQL injection, cross-site scripting (XSS), and cross-site request forgery (CSRF), many contemporary frameworks offer built-in security elements, including input validation. Maintaining current with your tools, libraries, and dependencies helps you to prevent security gaps. Using APIs or cloud storage also should be done with appropriate environment variables and authentication keys to prevent hardcoding sensitive data into your project.

Setting up your development environment also requires careful consideration of teamwork. Many times, developers work in teams; hence, productivity depends on a development environment designed for group projects. Here is where containerization techniques like Docker help to let teams share whole set ups. Developers should also make sure they are managing development, staging, and production branches using a cooperative workflow, including appropriate branching techniques like GitFlow, which employs issue trackers such as Jira or GitHub problems to help developers properly arrange their work. Since developers spend a lot of time in their development environment, making it as pleasant and effective as feasible can help to increase output. Using color schemes, keyboard shortcuts, and code snippets to customize your IDE or text editor will help ease reading and writing code friction. Task managers, note-taking programs, and project boards let developers stay on target and orderly. Using integrated tools for documentation—like Storybook for UI components or Swagger for API documentation—you can clearly present your work to others. Developers can concentrate on what counts most—building and enhancing the product—by means of effective and customized surroundings.

The tools and technology at hand for developers change along with the development world. Rising cloud-based development environments have been one of the most noticeable trends of late. With all required tools and dependencies pre-configured, these environments let developers operate in isolated and consistent surroundings. Cloud-based IDEs available on sites such as GitHub Codespaces, Gitpod, and Replit can be accessible from any device with an internet connection. This relieves developers of the requirement to set up their local workstations so they may rapidly enter coding free from environmental set up concerns. Remote work and team development, where teams may operate in real time anywhere, depend especially on these cloud IDEs since they enable cooperation.

Additionally, easily integrated with cloud deployment tools, cloud-based environments help developers release their code to production. Developers might, for example, create and test their code in a cloud environment and then directly implement it in AWS, Azure, or Google Cloud. By means of this integration, the development-to-deployment pipeline is streamlined, therefore minimizing the time required for local environment set up and guaranteeing consistent code performance during all development phases. Furthermore, common in cloud-based development platforms are built-in version control integration, which facilitates change management and teamwork among other developers.

Though they provide great ease and accessibility, cloud-based development environments are not without difficulties. One possible drawback is that cloud-based systems sometimes mostly rely on internet connection. Developers could have problems with latency or might be unable to access their development environment totally without a consistent connection. Moreover, cloud-based solutions could not support all the capabilities local environments offer and occasionally give less customizing choices. In a cloud-based setting, for instance, doing intensive computing chores could be slower than on a strong local system. Consequently, the particular requirements of the project and the development team will help one decide between cloud-based and local development environments.

Development of a mobile app, for example, calls for the installation of platform-specific tools such as Xcode for iOS development or Android Studio for Android development. Both instruments offer a spectrum of tools catered especially for mobile development, including emulators and simulators that let developers test their apps on virtual devices. Establishing these environments also entails configuring SDKs (Software Development Kits) and guaranteeing that the relevant dependent versions are installed. For iOS development, this also entails owning a Mac computer since macOS runs Xcode. Analogous set up of particular cross-compilers, debuggers, and other tools enabling code to be authored and compiled for embedded devices is also necessary for the development of embedded systems. Often more complex, these configurations call for a range of extra hardware or software tools beyond standard development environments.

Infrastructure as code (IaC) has grown to be a necessary component of creating development environments for teams and companies engaged in major projects. By use of code, IaC lets developers automatically create and manage infrastructure, therefore guaranteeing consistency and repeatability of environments. This method is often used in cloud systems where developers may specify, in configuration files, the resources they require—such as virtual machines, storage, or networking. Versioned, shared, and replicated across environments, tools including Terraform, AWS CloudFormation, and Ansible let developers code their infrastructure. This automation guarantees constant configuration of production, staging, and development environments and lowers the possibility of human mistakes in setting up surroundings.

Moreover, Docker and other containerizing technologies have transformed the way programmers arrange their workspace. Docker guarantees that an application operates reliably across several contexts by letting developers pack apps and all of their dependencies into isolated containers. Run on any machine, independent of the underlying operating system, containers are lightweight, and This makes it simple to test programs across several platforms free from concern for compatibility problems. Furthermore, easily integrates with orchestration technologies like Kubernetes, which can control container deployment, scaling, and networking in production environments Docker also manages. Since everyone is working with the same containerized environment, Docker can help teams working on challenging projects with several dependencies reduce environment set up and greatly ease collaboration.

Setting up a development environment usually consists of creating a local server and a database system for web developers. Setting up a local development environment for back-end developers using Node.js usually entails installing Node.js and npm (Node Package Manager) to handle dependencies. Then, frameworks like Express.js can be deployed to offer developing RESTful APIs middleware and routing capability. Tools like Webpack or Parcel let front-end developers pack HTML, CSS, and JavaScript files into ideal assets for deployment. Creating a front-end development environment could also entail configuring a local server, say using React, Angular, or Vue.js or the live-server package for static webpages. Every framework provides unique tools and set ups for designing, testing, and implementing projects.

Tracking the performance of their apps in real time, monitoring technologies including New Relic, Datadog, and Sentry, notify developers of problems including poor response times, memory leaks, or production faults. Integrated into the development environment, these instruments allow one to monitor performance all through the lifetime of the application. Using code analysis tools such as ESLint or Prettier to guarantee that code is clean, maintainable, and follows best standards also helps to optimize performance. These instruments can be included in the development environment to find possible problems before they start to affect manufacturing.

Making sure your development environment is thoroughly recorded is also crucial. For developers working in the environment, particularly new to the project or during team turnover, documentation is absolutely essential for reference. Recording the settings, dependencies, and any special set ups guarantees that every team member may quickly recreate the surroundings. It also supports the long-term maintainability of the project and helps newly hired developers onboard rapidly. Details on how to set up the environment, install dependencies, and run the project locally should all find a place in the documentation. Documenting development environments generally involves using Markdown or Wiki pages, which give developers easily available, unambiguous guidelines.

CHAPTER II

Core JavaScript Concepts for Beginners

Variables, Data Types, and Operators

Within programming, variables, data types, and operators are the basic building elements. These are the fundamental ideas enabling programmers to form logical structures in their programs and control data. Learning any programming language—including JavaScript—requires an awareness of how each of these element's functions. Variables hold values that one can access or change throughout the program running. Data types provide the kinds of data that can be kept in these variables; operators are the symbols or keywords acting on values and variables.

Basically, a variable is a container with a value that may be accessed and changed all through the program. Variables in most programming languages—including JavaScript—are named such that they are readily found.

These names—or identities—follow particular guidelines to guarantee their clarity, straightforward nature, and grammatical correctness. For instance, a more fitting name than a general term like x would be userAge or total amount.

JavaScript declares variables with the let, const, or var keywords. While constant is used for variables that should remain constant throughout the program, the let keyword lets variables be reassociated to new values. Historically employed in JavaScript, the var keyword is now usually eschewed in favor of let and const due to its function-scoped character, which can lead to unanticipated problems. Since it promotes code stability and helps prevent unintentional reassignment, const is very crucial in contemporary JavaScript.

Because they define what kind of values can be kept in a variable and what actions can be conducted on that data, data types are a fundamental idea in programming. Among the various basic data types available in JavaScript are numbers, texts, Booleans, null, undefined, and objects. Every one of these forms has a particular function within a program. Numbers can be utilized for computations; they are numerical numbers—both floating-point and integer values. Strings are sequences of characters surrounded by quotations used in text modification. Often found in conditional statements and loops, Boolean—truth values, either true or false—are Whereas undefined denotes that a variable has been declared but has not been assigned a value, null is the deliberate absence of any object value. Conversely, objects are complicated data types that enable key-value pair storing of groups of linked values.

JavaScript's number data type can be applied to a broad spectrum of operations, including comparisons, arithmetic calculations, and more. When needed, JavaScript automatically converts between integers and floating-point numbers, which makes it flexible but also a possible cause of problems should the programmer be negligent with accuracy. One of the main things to grasp about numbers in JavaScript is that they are all kept as 64-bit floating-point values; hence, some computations may cause rounding problems. Working with very large or very small numbers or running operations requiring decimal points will especially help one to see this.

Still, another basic data type in JavaScript is strings. One defines a string by enclosing a series of characters inside single quotes (" ") or double quotations (" "). Though uniformity in their use is advised, JavaScript treats them as comparable. Furthermore, helpful for building dynamic strings are template literals encased in backticks (), which let expressions be included in strings. JavaScript's flexible strings let one manipulate them in many ways, including string concatenation, slicing, and searching. Convenient ways to change string values are offered by functions such as split(), toUpperCase(), and to lowercase().

Programming logic and decision-making depend much on Booleans. Conditional statements and loops help to regulate program flow by means of them. A Boolean expression lets developers decide, depending on whether a condition is satisfied, whether true or false. Among other things, Booleans find frequent application in if, else, and while expressions in JavaScript. An if statement might, for example, see if a variable is true or false prior to running a block of code. In JavaScript, false is likewise handled as false; therefore, it can be used to indicate a negative or absent condition.

The deliberate lack of any value or object is embodied by the null data type. It is not like undefined, which suggests a variable has not been given any value. Often used as a placeholder for variables meant to retain object references but are not yet assigned to any particular object, null is. Though they are commonly mistaken, knowing the distinction between null and undefined is crucial since they are separate ideas in JavaScript. Whereas undefined is automatically assigned to uninitialized variables, null is specifically allocated to a variable.

Since objects let creators aggregate similar values together, they are among the most potent data types available in JavaScript. An object is a set of key-value pairings whereby the value can be any data type, including other objects, arrays, or functions, and the key is a string (or symbol) acting as the identification. This makes it possible to build intricate data structures like human representation with properties such as name, age, and address. JavaScript objects are quite versatile, and their properties may be accessed with bracket notation (object['property']) or dot notation (object.property).

In JavaScript, arrays are a unique kind of object that holds arranged sets of values. Made with square braces ([]), they can hold values of any kind—including other arrays. In JavaScript, arrays are dynamic—that is, their size changes during running time. Push(), pop(), shift(), and unshift() are among the several built-in ways they allow one to change their contents. Commonly used for storing lists of values—such as numbers, characters, or objects—arrays are a necessary element in the toolset of a JavaScript developer.

In programming, operators carry out actions on variables and values. Whether for arithmetic computations, text concatenation, comparison, or logical operations, JavaScript operators handle data. Arithmetic, assignment, comparison, logical, and other operators abound in JavaScript.

Basic mathematical operations—addition, subtraction, multiplication, and division—are carried out using arithmetic operators. One of the few instances in JavaScript where operators behave differently depending on the data types of the operands, string concatenation can also be accomplished with the addition operator (+). Calculating the remainder of a division can be accomplished with the modulo operator (%) in many contexts, including verifying even or odd values. Squaring a number or computing powers is just two applications for the exponentiation operator (**).

Variable assignments are accomplished with assignment operators. Though there are various shorthand operators for combining assignments with arithmetic operations, the simplest assignment operator is the equals symbol (=). The += operator, for example, adds a value to an already-existing variable and subtracts another. These shorthand operators can help to simplify and clarify code. Two values are compared using comparison operators, which produce a Boolean answer, either true or false. This difference guarantees that your comparisons are valid and act as expected.

Logical operators, including && (AND), || (OR), and! (NOT), let programmers integrate several criteria inside a more intricate logical statement. Often employed in conditional statements and loops, these operators help to build more complex decision-making frameworks. JavaScript operators also comprise the ternary operator, a shorthand for an if-else expression. The ternary operator exhibits a form condition. Expression 1 is carried out if the condition is true; expression 2 is carried out otherwise. When used sensibly, this operator allows for succinct conditional statements that could help to make the code more legible and compact.

Apart from these fundamental operators, JavaScript has operators for working with objects and arrays, including the spread (...) and destructuring operators. Cloning or merging arrays and objects becomes simpler when the spread operator lets one unpack elements from an array or properties from an object. This adaptability, meantime, can cause unanticipated behavior in some circumstances. Type coercion is JavaScript's automatic conversion of one data type into another to enable an operation. This usually results from several kinds of involvement in an operation—for example, from concatenating a string with a number. Although, in some circumstances, JavaScript is simpler to use, if the programmer is not aware of the type of data being changed, this can cause minor problems.

Let x = "5"; let y = 10; let result = x + y; This operation will produce "510," as JavaScript converts the number 10 into a string and subsequently concatenates strings. Although not properly considered, this behavior could cause problems even though it might not be immediately clear to someone not familiar with type coercion in JavaScript.

Often advised to use the strict equality operator (===) instead of the loose equality operator (==) is to avoid unanticipated outcomes from type coercion. The stringent equality operator guarantees that the type and the value must be the same for the comparison to be true by not doing type coercion. Type coercion will cause 5 == '5' to return true, whereas 5 === '5' will return false since the types vary—one is a number, and the other is a string. Likewise, knowing the several data types and how they act in JavaScript guarantees that the correct operations are carried out and helps to guarantee more suitable usage of variables.

JavaScript's data types include one extra capability: constructors and prototypes let one create bespoke objects and classes. Prototypical based inheritance in JavaScript lets objects inherit properties and methods from other objects, therefore enabling code reuse and the building of more intricate constructions. JavaScript's object-oriented programming capabilities depend on this ability to let developers arrange their code into logical parts, lower redundancy, and create more scalable programs.

Modern JavaScript also makes use of fresh ideas, including modules and asynchronous programming, which provide fresh approaches to running and structuring code. Promoting maintainability and modularity, modules let code be broken out into smaller, reusable portions. Conversely, asynchronous programming lets developers manage asynchronous processes such as data fetching, file reading, and user interaction without freezing the user interface by letting code be non-blocking executed. Both of these ideas are absolutely necessary for the creation of dynamic web applications since they mostly depend on the efficient application of operators, data kinds, and variables.

New data types, operators, and syntactic sugar are added to streamline routine chores and raise developer productivity as JavaScript develops. Newer iterations of JavaScript, for example, have included symbols for generating unique, immutable values usable as object keys and BigInt for managing arbitrarily huge integers. These new tools give JavaScript developers more power and flexibility so they may manage a wider spectrum of use cases and enhance the performance of their apps.

Becoming a competent web developer depends on knowing the subtleties of JavaScript's data types and operators whether it's handling simple arithmetic with integers, text with strings, or Booleans.

Finally, fundamental JavaScript ideas that let developers handle and analyze data inside their applications are variables, data types, and operators. While data types define the type of values a program can utilize, variables offer the means to save and refer to values. Then, operators specify how those values might be mixed, compared, and changed. These elements, taken together, set the foundation for strong, useful, and effective online applications. Understanding each of these components fully helps developers avoid frequent mistakes and produce better, more dependable code that runs across a range of use situations.

Understanding variables, data types, and operators will only become more crucial as JavaScript develops and fresh capabilities are included into the language. These ideas are fundamental for mastering advanced JavaScript capabilities, including closures, promises, and classes, in addition to being essential for developing efficient code. Strong knowledge of JavaScript's data handling will enable developers to fully embrace the language to produce contemporary, interactive web experiences that please consumers and stimulate invention.

Control Structures

Control structures are essential tools in programming that enable the flow of execution dependent on conditions or actions carried out frequently to be guided. These systems enable the programmer to create dynamic and adaptable codes able to manage a range of conditions depending on the input or the environment. JavaScript's control structures are conditional statements like if, else, and switch. Control structures also comprise looping constructions such as for, while, and do-while.

Within the field of programming, among the control mechanisms most used are conditional statements. These decisions and executions help the software to make judgments and carry out different blocks of code depending on particular conditions. In JavaScript, the simplest type of conditional reasoning is the if statement. It establishes, from its assessment, whether a given condition is true or not. Should the condition prove to be valid, the code housed within the if block is executed. Should this prove untrue, the program will move to the next part of the code. Having this talent helps you to be able to engage in specific activities just when specific requirements are met. You could use an if statement to confirm the authentication status of the user and provide material relevant to the authentication status.

One of the most potent features of the if statement itself is its potential to be coupled with an else block. Should the condition within the if statement prove to be false, the else block runs. Under these conditions, should the first condition prove unsatisfactory, the program is allowed to engage in an alternative set of actions. In a system letting users log in, for example, you could use an if statement to find out whether the user submitted the suitable credentials. Should the user be able to log in successfully, access will be allowed; otherwise, an otherwise block error message will show up.

Apart from the usual if and otherwise statements, JavaScript also offers the else if clause, which lets several conditions be checked in consecutive sequence. The language gains from this clause really nicely. When there are several unusual options that must be assessed and handled individually, this comes in really handy. Once every conditional statement is completed, the program would decide whether the score falls within a given range and then assign the appropriate grade depending on that exact range.

Still, another important control element linked with JavaScript is the switch statement. The switch statement is a substitute for many if-else if chains when you need to test a single variable against several different values. The switch statement is simpler and more readable in cases when a lot of conditions must be verified. An expression is evaluated, and then the outcome of that evaluation is matched with every case value included within the switch block. It runs the code related to a match it finds right away. Should no match prove to be found, the backup plan will be followed. When you have to look for certain values of a variable, the switch statement is rather useful. The switch statement can help you, for instance, manage menu choices, routing settings, or various tasks inside an application.

Once the program's flow under control, depending on the needs, has been under control, it could also be required for it to execute repetitious duties. By now, loop structures have started to matter in the debate. Loops are a basic component of the programming language of choice for actions requiring repetition, such as iterating over elements in an array or constantly querying the user for input until proper data is supplied. JavaScript has three distinct types of loops: for, while, and do-while.

The most often utilized kind of loop in JavaScript projects could be the for loop. Usually, it is used in scenarios when the number of repeats is known in advance. Before the start of the loop, one runs the initialization phase just once. The condition is verified to be true before starting every iteration. If so, the loop runs the code contained within the specified block. Every iteration ends with the increment/decrement step carried performed, therefore updating the loop variable. This structure is a great fit in circumstances when you have to iterate a certain number of times, say when processing elements in an array or doing repeated over and over again calculations.

Conversely, the while loop is used in cases when exact prior knowledge of the iteration count is unknown. Rather, the loop will keep running for as long as a certain condition is assessed to produce a positive value. This makes the while loop helpful in situations where the program must repeat an activity until a particular condition is satisfied. Unlike the for loop, the while loop depends on the condition to decide when to close the loop; it does not have an increment or decrement step specifically included in the structure of the loop.

Independent of whether or not the condition is discovered to be false at the start of the loop, the code included within the do-while loop is run at least once. The condition of a do-while loop is evaluated following the running of the included code. This helps to explain this. Cases when it is required to guarantee that the body of the loop is executed at least once, say when the user is being requested for input, in a way that guarantees they are asked at least once, regardless of the beginning state.

Whether or not the condition of the loop is still true, the break statement results in an instantaneous loop quieter. This is quite useful if you want to stop looping once a given condition has been met. Conversely, the continuous statement will go to the next iteration instead of the one the loop is now running. Every one of these two remarks gives the programmer total control over the way loops are executed.

When working with more complicated reasoning, such as nested loops or conditional blocks, careful monitoring of the flow of execution is absolutely vital. This is so because these kinds of reasoning might be really complex. Because they result in an increase in the complexity of the program's logic, nested loops—loops contained inside other loops—can be especially difficult to control. Of great relevance is knowledge of the interactions among control structures and the means of changing the flow of execution at every level. Using comments and the right indentation helps one keep nested structures legible and maintained.

Current JavaScript not only offers these basic control structures but also enables more complex features, such asynchronous control flow. Asynchronous programming is a necessary element of web development since it lets JavaScript manage chores, including collecting data from a server, reading files, or waiting for user input without freezing the user interface. JavaScript's asynchronous and wait keywords enable developers to create asynchronous code that looks and operates exactly as synchronous application code. This helps one to work with asynchronous activities and preserve a clear and logical flow of control at the same time.

Control structures are, then, the basic building blocks of JavaScript applications. These systems let builders control the flow of execution depending on tasks repeated and situations. Conditional statements like if, else, and switch help one make decisions; repeating actions is made feasible by loops like for, while, and do-while. The JavaScript programming language offers a whole set of capabilities for controlling code running. Among other capabilities, these tools comprise break, continue, and asynchronous control flow approaches. Modern web development demands a strong grasp of these control structures if one wants to create code that is not only efficient, readable, and manageable but also able to handle a broad spectrum of scenarios.

Functions and Scope

The field of programming depends on the ideas of functions and scope; they also help to produce code that is modular, highly efficient, and easy to maintain. Programmers have access to several tools, and among them JavaScript functions are among the most flexible. These technologies help developers improve code organization, capture capability, and lower repetition by means of encapsulating functionality. Among the strongest instruments you have at hand are these ones. When we discuss a function in its most basic form, we imply a chunk of code that may be reused and intended for a certain task. Developers can write code only once and then use it numerous times by using functions, therefore removing the necessity for constant rewriting of the same logic. This does away with the need to repeatedly present the same reasoning. This helps the code to be more easily maintained as well as to improve its readability. One's functions are ones that enable one to get inputs, act depending on those inputs, and subsequently return the outcomes of those activities. This kind of encapsulating logic helps to make the codebase more structured and helps to minimize the clutter in the main body of code by so capturing it. Better organization in huge systems, where logic can get ever more complicated, depends on the ability to group related code under a meaningful name. This capacity helps companies to be more effective. This is especially true in situations linked with general usage.

The program is in charge of calling or activating functions whenever they are needed to complete a particular chore. A function call starts the execution of that function. The function was called under the name of a reference to the piece of code it reflects. Arguments are the values or variables handed into a function, as it is called. Arguments take on a purpose. One important quality of a function is its ability to welcome arguments. If given these inputs, functions can perform operations on a broad spectrum of data without explicitly being connected to particular values. Functions are incredibly flexible and fit for a wide range of use cases since they let arguments pass throughout their execution. This is so resulting from their given independence. Establishing a mechanism that would let one carry out a mathematical computation is one instance of this. When the function is called with the intention of performing the computation, the integers engaged in it would be given to it as arguments.

Realizing the scope of the problem could be more difficult, even if the functions themselves are not too difficult to grasp. In the context of the code, this is known as the "scope" of a variable or function. It is the background against which the function or variable is accessible. It is a basic concept to control the lifespan of variables and functions inside a program as well as to prevent name conflicts or mistakes generated by variable overwriting. Furthermore, required is the control of the lifespan of functions and variables. Two forms of scope that define how variables are scoped and how they may be accessed are functional scope and block scope. There is use for both of these kinds of scope. JavaScript defines two types of scopes: one for this and another for others.

Function-scoped variables are those declared in JavaScript in line with the var syntax. Declared with the var keyword, a variable can be accessible all around the function in which it is defined, including any nested blocks housed inside that function. This is practical as the var keyword guarantees the accessibility of the variable. For instance, any code contained within a function is able to access a variable specified inside of that function. This holds whether the code is housed in a block or a loop. One should pay great attention to this. This absence of block scope in loops or conditional statements sometimes causes unanticipated behavior. This is especially valid while dealing with conditional statements. One instance of this would be the risk that variables defined inside a loop could unintentionally become accessible outside of that loop, therefore causing code faults.

Conversely, variables declared using let and const clauses are those that are thought of as block-scoped variables. This suggests that they are just reachable inside the particular block of code in which they are defined—that is, within a function, an if statement, or a loop. Stated otherwise, they are exclusively available within the framework of the block of code in which they are defined. This more thorough scoping allows one to minimize the unwanted access to variables not in line with their intended use. This results in a simpler code for which one has less chance of including mistakes. Block-scoped variables help to guarantee that the lifespan of a variable is limited to the particular block in which it was defined.

As a result, when and where variables are accessible, controlling them is much easier.

The idea of scope and closures—which arise when a function keeps having access to variables from its outside scope even after the execution of that outer scope has been completed—have a close relationship. This is a case study of how closure relates to the idea of scope. JavaScript lets functions retain the background in which they were created so they might be used going forward. JavaScript's powerful ability to let functions recall this environment is closures. One function stated inside another generates a closure with the variables of the function defined outside of it. The two functions define one another inside each other, therefore forming this closure. This is why the inner function is allowed to access and change those variables even after the outside function has been run. JavaScript-written programs make extensive use of closures for a range of uses, including callbacks, control of asynchronous functions, and the creation of private variables. Furthermore, numerous additional apps make use of closures. Moreover, they are crucial for event handlers or timers, which depend on the context in which the function was developed to be maintained. The ability of a function depends on these elements.

Working with functions and scope in JavaScript calls for one of the most important issues to address in terms of the execution environment. The execution context is the surroundings a function performs its execution. Although it is in charge of defining the values of variables, it also helps to ascertain the program's status at a certain moment in time. Every time a function is called, a new execution context is generated and distinguished by its special scope. This context generates a whole fresh execution environment. The invocation of a function produces the function obtaining its own special collection of local variables unrelated to any other instances of the same function being invoked. This suggests that no other function in the system might be shared from the variables. Separating every function call guarantees that each function call is carried out independently and helps to avoid conflicts between variables used in several invocations when they are utilized in distinct contexts.

Global scope is another very necessary component of scope used in JavaScript. Declared in the global scope, a variable can be accessed from anywhere inside the program. This means that every function or block of code in the program can be referenced and changed from inside the program itself. Although this could seem to be a simple technique, the existence of global variables could cause name conflicts. This is particularly true in big systems when several developers are concurrently working on the same codebase. Reducing the use of global variables and restricting the scope of their application is a tactic that is advised in order to lower the possibility of negative side effects. This activity is done to lessen the risks connected to the globally spreading global variables. When it comes to the process of encapsulating variables and functions, developers generally apply techniques including closures and module patterns. One of the advantages of this is that it helps to ensure that these elements are not unnecessarily subjected to global reach.

JavaScript can also handle higher order operations. Using higher-order functions helps one to get a significant degree of freedom in terms of the organization and implementation of codes. JavaScript's array tools, for example, exhibit higher-order functions. Map, filter, and reduce algorithms are more instances of higher-order functions. These techniques not only have callback purposes but also work on arrays in a visually appealing and declarative manner. Particularly in the paradigms of functional programming, higher-order functions are applied somewhat regularly within the field of JavaScript.

In functional programming paradigms, particularly, this is true.

Furthermore, linked to functions is the concept of recursion, which is also rather significant. A recursive function is one of those which calls itself to address a problem. This kind of ability seeks a solution to the dilemma. Recursion is a great tactic being used right now to divide difficult issues into smaller, more manageable sub-problems. Recursion can be used in several ways to reduce the code count, therefore simplifying and improving reading ease. Conversely, recursion calls for rigorous control of the base case, therefore stopping the function from calling itself indefinitely. Recursion is a recursive programming method; hence this is so. Often employed in JavaScript for a variety of tasks, recursion is a technique.

Asynchronous programming is essential for the construction of websites since numerous operations—including network queries, user interactions, and file I/O—need to wait for external events to complete before proceeding to the next level. Sometimes, functions must keep access to variables from their outside scope even after the outer function has finished dealing with asynchronous processes. This is so since asynchronous events are more likely. Closures become quite important at this stage since they enable asynchronous functions to access and modify variables from the context in which they were generated. This is so because closures let the functions access and change variables even in cases of later execution.

One of the most important difficulties one can run over while working with JavaScript functions and scope is keyword management. This keyword denotes the object running the present code that is under operation. Therefore, the value of this depends on the way the function is called, so it is quite essential to have a strong awareness of how this works in a variety of conditions in order to prevent difficulties. This relates to the global object (or undefined in strict mode) in the framework of a normal function, but in the framework of methods, it relates to the object the method owner is. Stated differently, the object that forms the method is the global one. It is possible for the value of this to develop more complex when functions are carried out in event handling or as callbacks. This is entirely within reach. JavaScript lets developers use explicit control over the value of this by means of binding, calling, and applying techniques. These all-around strategies are meant to assist in problem-solving for developers.

Key ideas that let developers create modular, controllable, and efficient code are JavaScript's functions and scope. Drawing from the information given above, this is the conclusion one can reach. This is so because they can better control the extent of the project. The two elements that define JavaScript programming fundamentally are functionality and scope. By using this basis, developers may preserve a clean and orderly codebase while also designing complex and interactive web apps using their foundation. Apart from closures, recursion, and higher-order functions—which provide even more complexity to the possibilities of functions—the interaction between functions and scope is dynamic. This adds to the reality that these characteristics offer even more complexity. JavaScript developers who have a strong grasp of these few ideas will be able to produce robust apps that are also easily maintained and scaled.

Arrays and Objects

JavaScript has two basic data structures known as objects and arrays. Many more programming employment are based on these frameworks. Developers who deal with JavaScript must have both of these tools at hand since arrays and objects both have significant roles in the process of storing and arranging data. Developing complex applications requires a strong awareness of how these structures work, how they vary from one another, and how best to use them. The concept of arrays and objects will be discussed in this section together with their usefulness and the relevance of object and array interactions in JavaScript programming.

The array is among the data structures used in JavaScript the most often. The basic building components of arrays are a set of values. Any data type—texts, objects, integers, even other arrays—can be found among these values. There might be numbers, for instance. An array is a data structure enabling the storage of many items inside one variable. This is quite useful while handling several enormous volumes of data. Unlike simple variables, which only retain one value, arrays allow one to compile in an organized manner data related to one another.

JavaScript allows an array to be indexed, therefore assigning a numerical position to every value within the array starting with zero. This index enables developers to access certain elements kept within the array. Using indices to get the elements of the array will help you to handle massive datasets in a simple and effective manner. Should an array contain a list of names, for example, developers can access every name by consulting the index that each name occupies within the array. The first name will be allocated a zero index, the second name an index of one, and so on to the third name. Using arrays, one may accomplish a great range of tasks, including data sorting, item addition and removal, and computation over several elements. One finds great adaptability in arrays.

There are several built-in methods in the JavaScript programming language that let one work on arrays. Similarly, the shift() and unshift() tools let users add or delete entries from the start of an array based on their tastes. These methods provide developers more freedom by allowing them to change arrays as needed throughout the running of the program.

Still, another great benefit of arrays in JavaScript is their capacity to store data of many kinds. Unlike the usual use of arrays, which are meant to store groups of similar objects, JavaScript arrays do not impose any restrictions on the data types of components. This suggests that thanks to this capacity, programmers can store objects, strings, and integers inside one array. When dealing with heterogeneous data or when the data types might vary throughout the program's running, this adaptability could prove extremely helpful.

Although arrays provide a handy way to keep sorted data, objects fulfill the same function but give more structural freedom. Data can be conveniently kept in arrays. Objects in JavaScript are collections of key-value pairs, in which every key is a string (or symbol), and every value may be any data type—including arrays and even other objects. One can also refer to items as groups of objects. By use of objects, developers can store more complex data than depending just on number indices. Associations between values and descriptive keys help one to achieve this. Objects are particularly suited for depicting items in the real world that have several various characteristics or properties because of their construction.

Consider an object that substitutes for a human, for example. Among the traits that might be found in the object are name, age, address, and email address. Every one of these qualities would save a different bit of personal knowledge about the person. Objects that make use of meaningful attribute names (keys) help one to arrange related data in an evident and simple manner. This varies greatly from arrays, where the lack of descriptive keys might make it more difficult to understand the role of the data.

Objects also help developers to work with more complex data structures because of their great degree of flexibility. Arrays can be used, for example, as values inside an object therefore enabling the creation of nested data structures. This capacity is especially useful when working with hierarchical or nested data since it facilitates more effective operation. A student's object might be a set of courses, each of which is an object in its own right with properties including the courseName and the grade. The capacity to nest objects and arrays concurrently helps developers to efficiently create complex data structures.

One of the most important benefits of objects is their potential to save values using descriptive keys. Working with large datasets or data from outside sources, including application programming interfaces (APIs), comes in really helpful. Meaningful keys free developers from depending on numerical indices, which might be prone to mistakes, as they enable them to easily access certain bits of data. This lets programmers save work and time. This makes objects especially suited for circumstances in which the structure of the data is more complex and requires adaptability.

Furthermore, crucial in JavaScript is a strong knowledge of the relationship linking objects and arrays. While objects are usually used to represent more complex objects, arrays are usually used for storing ordered collections of data. Still, there are also different ways that objects and arrays might be mixed. For instance, an object might have arrays, and an array could have objects. JavaScript allows developers to mix and match arrays and objects, therefore allowing them to show data in the most appropriate way for the current use case.

Though they have some commonalities, arrays, and objects differ greatly in many important respects. One significant difference is how easily they might be obtained. Numerical indices help one to access objects in arrays; in objects, values are retrieved by use of keys. Arrays are, therefore, perfectly suited for sorted collections, in which the position of every member is of great importance, given their contrast. Conversely, objects are more suited for depicting unordered sets of key-value pairs in which the relationships among the data have more relevance than their sequence in the collection.

Still, another major difference is the way arrays and objects are iterated over. Loops allow developers to cycle over the elements in arrays; the for or for each approach is, therefore, rather common in this process. As arrays are sorted, developers may rely on the index to access every element in the array in the right sequence. Objects, on the other hand, are collections devoid of any particular sequence, so the keys do not have a predefined arrangement. Developers often iterate over an object using tools like Object.keys() or Object.entries() in common sense. These techniques help developers to retrieve the key-value pairs connected with the object. Although both arrays and objects can be iterated, the ways in which one approaches and uses them differ because of their inherent structures.

Arrays and objects differ from one another in terms of performance as well as certain characteristics. When it comes to the storing and retrieval of ordered groupings of data, arrays shine remarkably; the techniques designed for them for changing elements are quite successful. Conversely, objects are made to be the best fit for storing key-value pairs. They particularly work well in cases when the relationship between the data is more important than the data storage sequence. Because of their intrinsic data representation, arrays may consume more memory than objects in general. Conversely, when it comes to storing intricate data structures, objects usually have better memory efficiency.

Although JavaScript makes great use of both arrays and objects, and they are both rather flexible, the choice of data structure to use depends on the specific needs of the application. Arrays are among the most appropriate data structures to utilize for ordered collections of data—such as lists or queues—where the position of every item is important. Objects are the ideal option when depicting real-world entities with different characteristics, particularly in cases when the relationships between the data are more crucial than the data order. Constructing more complex data structures usually requires developers to join arrays and objects, which is basic knowledge. This is done to make use of the features any kind of data structure offers.

Two of the most important data structures JavaScript has to provide, I would want to say are arrays and objects. Unlike objects, which allow flexibility in terms of storing key-value pairs, arrays provide a quick way to save ordered sets of data concurrently. JavaScript developers must have a firm awareness of how to make excellent use of arrays and objects since these are basic elements in the process of creating dynamic and robust apps. Unlike arrays, which are ideal for presenting ordered data, objects are more appropriate for depicting complex entities that exist in the real world and have several attributes. Combining arrays and objects allows developers to create quite dynamic and adaptable data structures. Two of the most useful instruments in the JavaScript toolset are arrays and objects. They apply whether your task involves simple lists or complex hierarchical data.

CHAPTER III

Interacting with the Browser and DOM

The Document Object Model (DOM)

An indispensable element that makes it possible for guests to interact with web pages is the Document Object Model (DOM). It is a basic idea in web development and offers a major help during the process. Designed as a programming interface for web documents, the Document Object Model (DOM) shows the framework of a web page in a way that programs might change. Most of the improvements that programs can bring about are achieved by using JavaScript programming language. It is therefore, an essential part of the web development that is being done since it helps developers to make dynamic changes to the content and architecture of a web page. Since the Document Object Model (DOM) connects the interactive and dynamic behavior made possible by scripting languages with the static HTML markup of a page, it is impossible to overestimate its relevance in the process of building websites. This link is crucial since it makes websites possible to grow.

Designed to help explain the structure of the document, the Document Object Model (DOM) is a hierarchical model showing its construction as a tree of nodes. Nodes are objects that line up with page portions, such as elements, characteristics, or text. Every node is like an object. Essential in the document is the Document Object Model (DOM). Programming languages, including JavaScript, can make use of the Document Object Model (DOM) in order to acquire access to, change, and delete elements and material included within the document. Web pages can become interactive and responsive to user activities, including clicks, form inputs, and keyboard inputs, only by interaction between the user and the page. It is this interaction that allows web pages to react to user behavior. Without the Document Object Model (DOM), the World Wide Web would be restricted to static sites with no dynamic content changes accessible.

Language-independent means that, although the Document Object Model (DOM) is most usually used in concert with JavaScript in web development, it is not limited to any one programming language. This is so since the DOM is not based on any one programming language. It allows developers to access and change the structure of a webpage by means of programming, therefore enabling them to alter the content, add elements, remove elements, and change the style. Still, other characteristics include style modification capability. Using the Document Object Model (DOM), developers can, for example, change the content within a paragraph. They might also edit the content of a paragraph, rearrange a page by adding or deleting parts, and update the source of an image. Modern web applications need material altered in real time without requiring a full page reload. These applications depend on this dynamic aspect of the Document Object Model (DOM) since it lets materials be changed in real time.

One of the key differences between the Document Object Model (DOM) and other forms is the tree structure, which reflects the structure of a web page. The document object, which relates to the whole HTML document, will be found right at the start of the tree here. Branches that stretch from the document object reflect several elements of the document, including the HTML>, head>, and body> and we call these branches. Every one of these components could contain child nodes—that is, representations of the siblings incorporated inside them. One can occur with this. The body element, which will contain child nodes reflecting various elements (such as paragraphs, graphics, and divisions) on the page, is one instance of this. The hierarchical approach of the document makes it simple for developers to negotiate. This framework helps them to negotiate the document by allowing them to access any element of the page depending on its relationship to other elements of the tree.

By means of a consistent collection of techniques and properties, the page object model (DOM) enables interaction with the structure of the page. This lets one interact with the page. These methods let developers create new nodes, access some existing ones, and change those ones. They also let designers create fresh nodes. For example, the getElementById() method may be used to get an element depending on its unique ID, while the getElementsByTagName() method can be used to obtain all elements belonging to a given type. Both of these techniques are among several that one can apply. Once a certain element has been identified, the DOM techniques can be applied to change both its properties and content. Once the element is known, this is feasible. Developers have the flexibility to adjust the content included inside an element by using the innerHTML property.

One can make real time modifications to a web page by adjusting the Document Object Model (DOM), which allows dynamic interactions with users. This holds for dynamic as well as stationary interactions. JavaScript allows one to identify events occurring on a web page, including those involving user clicks of buttons or form submission. Furthermore, changes to the document object model (DOM) can follow these actions. This makes it possible to create very dynamic web apps that can react to user input without requiring the page to be shown once more. In the case of a form, for instance, user input can be verified in real time, and error warnings are either shown or hidden depending on the entered information. The way forms are built makes this feasible. The content of a page can also be changed dynamically, as shown by the previous illustration. The ability to put fresh content onto a blog and update a shopping cart in real time would be two instances of this.

Furthermore, there are methods for managing events—that is, those activities or events occurring within the browser program. Events from the computer abound in clicks on the mouse, keyboard inputs, and page loading. The DOM offers this series of techniques. Web development depends on event handling since it helps creators specify particular activities that should be done anytime a user interacts with a page. This is so because event handling lets programmers specify what should be done. A developer wishing to add an event listener to a button meant to wait for a click event to signal that it is present would be exhibiting this. Should the button be pressed, the event listener will initiate a callback mechanism suitably. This feature's ability to accomplish a range of tasks—such as changing the website's content, forwarding data to the server, or running an animation—allows one to do Thanks to the application of this event-driven approach, it is now possible to create very engaging and responsive user interfaces.

Comprising several elements, the Document Object Model (DOM) is most importantly enabled by its capacity to enable asynchronous actions. Modern web development is typical for web applications to interact with off-site servers in order to gather data or perform background functions without disturbing the user interface. This helps to expedite the process of creating webpages. This makes internet apps seem to be more like native programs.

The idea of DOM manipulation performance is another basic topic linked to the Document Object Model (DOM). Although the Document Object Model (DOM) is a useful instrument for dynamically updating web pages, it is important to examine the performance consequences of frequent changes in the DOM. This is so as the document object model includes the DOM. The browser is required to update its internal page view; every element is changed as the Document Object Model (DOM) is an in-memory form of the HTML document. The DOM runs in memory; hence this is so. Should a lot of DOM activities be executed in quick succession, performance issues could arise, especially for web pages with more volume. To solve this problem, developers use strategies such as batching DOM changes, minimizing direct DOM access, and using virtual DOM in systems like React, so increasing efficiency. We address the problem using these techniques.

A major progress in the process of changing the digital document (DOM) is the introduction of the virtual DOM idea. Several Tools and Frameworks developed in the JavaScript programming language make use of the lightweight clone of the real DOM, the virtual Document Object Model (DOM). This helps the performance to be better. Comparatively to the real DOM, the process of comparing the virtual DOM is called "reconciliation," and it occurs anytime the virtual DOM is altered. Minimizing the number of updates helps the real DOM to be more efficient since only the variations between the two apply to it. One applies just the variations between the two. This approach is very helpful in situations where the page state is often altered. A single-page application (SPA) is one type of such application since it lets the whole page be changed without having the page fully refreshed.

Though JavaScript is the language primarily used for interacting with the Document Object Model (DOM), there are other languages that also provide techniques to deal with the DOM. Among these languages is TypeScript. Designed especially to interact with the Document Object Model (DOM), TypeScript is a superset of JavaScript with static typing among its capabilities. With its support, one can complete the production of less complicated to maintain and more error-resistant codes. TypeScript gives developers further tools to enable them to create more precisely and effectively written code. These instruments are applied in the interaction with aspects of the Document Object Model (DOM). Two instances of these several uses are type checking and interfaces. Therefore, it is especially helpful while working on complicated programs or large codebases since it guarantees that the required types are being applied and lowers the possibility of issues arising when running. This is so because it ensures the suitable use of the relevant kinds.

One of the difficulties developers encounter when working with the Document Object Model (DOM) is guaranteeing compatibility using a range of browsers. Although the Document Object Model (DOM) is a common specification, browsers could use it in somewhat different ways depending on one another. This may cause variations in the way a website is shown or in the way interactions are handled. Often, developers must utilize polyfills or frameworks like jQuery to standardize the behavior of the Document Object Model (DOM) across several browsers. This is so because DOM's behavior could differ depending from browser to browser. Polyfills are scripts used to provide behavior consistent across current browsers or to offer capability absent in past browsers. These scripts help consumers to reach both of these objectives. Using polyfills allows developers to ensure that their web pages will operate correctly across a broad spectrum of browsers with which they are working. Although the browser does not naturally enable some features, this is nevertheless technically possible.

Regarding web development, the Document Object Model (DOM) is a concept regarded as being absolutely crucial. By means of this method, developers can interact with and change the framework of online pages in real time. It is feasible for developers to create dynamic and interactive websites and applications by means of a consistent approach for accessing, modifying, and updating HTML elements. Even if online applications are still under development, the Document Object Model (DOM) will always be a crucial part of contemporary web building. This results from the ability of developers to create interactive, rich, responsive user experiences.

Event Handling

In web development especially in JavaScript, where it serves as the mechanism for reacting to user interactions with a web page or application, event handling is a basic idea. As stated, event handling is the process of enabling a web page or application to function. Stated differently, the development of a website mostly depends on event management since it is its pillar. Usually referred to as events, these interactions comprise loading the website, clicking the mouse, and pushing the keys. One could find instances of these interactions using mouse clicks. Event handling is the technique by which developers respond to these events by means of specific capability or behavior.

Professionals in event management handle this responsibility. This approach helps one to make websites dynamic and interactive. This is a necessary quality since it helps to create responsive and reactive in real time user interfaces that respond to the inputs the user provides. The user will thus enjoy an experience that is not only fascinating but also easily understandable. Creating functioning yet also responsive and user-friendly websites and applications calls for effective event handling. In the current web development environment, this is a necessary element of the process of building websites and applications.

An event in JavaScript is an action or occurrence commenced by the user or the browser. Stated otherwise, an event will transpire. An event can also result from the person themself. These occurrences could range from a user hitting a button to a page totally loaded to a form being entered. These events all make sense. More usually known as an event handler, the activation of a callback function occurs automatically following an event. This ability helps to decide the next actions to be done should the occurrence of an issue transpires. Thus, event handling is a very important element when it comes to guaranteeing that the application responds in real time to activities done by the user, such as filling in a form, interacting with a button, or entering data into a field. This is so because the application real timely records user actions. Web programs would remain fixed and unable to react to user comments if event handling was not included in them. As a result, the uses would get far less interactive and fascinating.

Within the field of JavaScript, there are many distinct kinds of events that one can control; each of these events relates to a particular kind of user interaction. Typical events comprise click events, mouse events, keyboard events, form events, and window events. These are all instances of something thought to be ordinary. Click events follow when a user clicks on a component—a button or link. These events point to a clicked component. Events create themselves whenever the mouse moves, presses, or releases a specific element. We call these occurrences mouse events. This allows one to have exact control over the way an element reacts to user input and to get better flexibility all through the design process. Anytime a user pushes or releases keys on the keyboard, keyboard events are produced. This makes it reasonable to record and react to particular key presses. Every key a user presses, or releases on the keyboard sets off a keyboard event. In many different fields, including the handling of form submissions, the validation of data, and the interactions between form elements, form events are especially crucial. Window events are activities linked to the browser window itself that enable the handling of several actions. Among these include moving the window to another size, scrolling, and loading a page.

Event handling in JavaScript can be done in several methods; generally, it is the process of spotting an event with a certain element housed within the website. Event listeners or event characteristics relate to the methods used in this regard. Currently the most often used and modern method for event management is using event listeners. This is so because event listeners enable developers to create an event handler code running whenever the event happens. JavaScript allows one to include event listeners into HTML elements. These listeners provide more degree of flexibility than event characteristics, which were usually used in early methods of web building. One can apply these listeners to HTML elements. The addEventListener approach helps one to add an event listener to an element. This method requires the user to indicate the type of event the listener will be listening for as well as the purpose this will serve anytime the event occurs. This approach offers a more modular and maintainable means of handling events than straight assigning events in HTML attributes like onclick or onmouseover. This is not at all like the method utilized in the past.

Event Properties and listeners differ significantly from one another. This is so because event attendees enable the linking of several purposes to a single event, hence providing more freedom and control over the handling of the events. Event properties allow an element in HTML to be connected with a single event handler code. This is plausible. This may cause the code to become less maintainable as well as to result in duplicate of it. On the other side, event listeners allow one to link several event handler techniques to the same event on the same element. Event listeners help one to achieve this. This also helps to improve the code's organization and lower process redundancy at the same time. As a result, event listeners have evolved into the preferred way of handling events in contemporary JavaScript.

Event delegation is one way used to control events more successfully. When objects are dynamically added or taken off the page, this approach is quite helpful. This is not only a fundamental idea in event management but also a key idea in event management. One alternative to the custom of clearly linking event listeners to every component is event delegation. Should an event transpire on a child element, it is passed up the DOM tree to the element acting as the parent of the child element. This is so because events are spread via the DOM hierarchy—DOM hierarchy—that an event occurring on a child element is successful. Establishing a link between a single event listener and a parent component enables developers to control events for many child components. This eliminates the need that the developers to link particular event listeners to every child element straight-forward. This approach is particularly helpful in cases when elements are added dynamically since it ensures that the event handling will remain efficient not only during the introduction of new elements but also during their dynamic presence.

Still, another basic idea in event management is event propagation. It speaks to the way events pass via the Document Object Model (DOM). Event propagation is the process by which, upon an event occurring on an element, another event is set off. We refer to this series of events as event propagation overall. There are steps within the process of event propagation known as bubbling and capturing. These two phases are involved. The event starts at the root of the page and then moves down the DOM tree until it reaches the element under focus when the capturing phase gets underway. This keeps on until the event gets to the element under focus. The event moves from the element under concentration to the root of the document object model (DOM) tree during the bubbling phase. This happens throughout the whole process. Events are spread in the algorithm's bubbling phase under the default set up. Once an event sets off its parent components will bubble up until it is especially stopped within the bubble. This is the situation right up until the event is specifically called off. Developers have the means to modify this behavior by applying techniques like stopPropagation and preventDefault. These techniques help the developers decide whether or not their default action is triggered and manage the way events spread.

Not only is the use of event handling restricted to human connections, but it also is rather important in the management of asynchronous operations. Among these background chores are file uploads, questions to the application programming interface (API), and other tasks. For instance, it is usual practice to employ event handling when a web application sends an AJAX request to a server to wait for the answer and subsequently change the user interface upon data acquisition. This is done so to provide a consistent user experience. In the same vein, event handling may be used to verify the form inputs before submission when a user interacts with a form. One can start this before the form is turned in. Real time user comments ensure that the data is accurate, thereby guaranteeing the correctness of the information. Event handling helps developers to react to asynchronous events as the completion of an API request or the submission of a form, therefore facilitating these kinds of interactions. The fact that event management makes these kinds of interactions feasible helps to enable this.

In the field of web development, event management is also a necessary element that greatly increases accessibility. Accessible web apps let those with impairments interact with the website by using a wide range of input devices, therefore enabling them to participate. This category includes, among other assistive technologies, keyboards, screen readers, and other devices. Effective event handling guarantees that all users—including those with disabilities—are able to negotiate and interact with web pages in a way that is not just user-friendly but also practical, therefore guaranteeing that this is practicable. For instance, keyboard events are vitally essential to enable guests to traverse a page without depending on anything like a mouse. Focus events, however, guarantee that keyboard shortcuts allow interactive objects to be chosen and triggered. Focus events help one to achieve this. Furthermore, developers can make use of event handling to guarantee that users of screen readers remain current on the most recent changes to dynamic content. Those with visual disabilities will so find it easier to engage in the event.

Regarding event planning, performance is also another crucial factor that has to be given thought. Although event handling allows web pages to have strong interactivity, it is important to ensure that event listeners do not compromise performance. This is so because audience members may affect performance negatively. This is particularly true for pages with high degrees of complexity and lots of interactive elements or interactions. Multiple event listeners coupled with a lot of elements provide a common performance problem in this regard. Consequently, too much RAM is used, which causes reaction times to drop. One of the strategies developers use to reduce the number of event attendees linked to particular objects is event delegation. Thanks to this help to developers, the found defects are corrected. Another method used to control the frequency of an event handler function activation is throttling. The execution of the function is restricted with this method. This helps to prevent the function from being called too often during operations like resizing or scrolling. When developers maximize the way events are handled, they can produce not only highly engaging but also quite efficient web apps.

Web development depends critically on event handling since it allows web pages and apps to react in real time to user interactions and other events occurring on the web. In essence, web development cannot exist without event management. By listening to particular events and implementing actions aligned with those events, developers can generate dynamic and interactive online experiences that engage users and offer great functionality. Developers can generate these events. JavaScript's event-handling capabilities—which cover a wide range of techniques and strategies—such as event listeners, event delegation, and event propagation—give developers the means to design responsive and user-friendly interfaces. Among these powers are those of event listeners, event delegation, and event dissemination. The need for good event management will only grow as the field of web development keeps growing. Therefore, good event management is a talent definitely needed for every web developer to have. Event handling is a key element of modern web development. Among the several aspects of event handling are those related to user input management, asynchronous process interaction, and assurance of accessibility. The application of this concept enables developers to create interactive and not only intriguing online apps.

Forms and User Input

Modern web development depends critically on forms and user input since they enable people to interact with websites in a way that is meaningful to them. By completing a form, users can provide information that serves as a means of access to engage in activities, including account creation, message forwarding for contact, or purchase making. User input—that is, the data entered by a user via a form—is text, numbers, dates, and even file uploads are just a few of the several ways you may gather this data. Building effective forms and processing user input in making user experience and guaranteeing that the data acquired is correct, safe, and handled in a suitable manner. Design, functionality, and validation of forms are fundamental aspects of web development.

Since it defines the structure and behavior of the form itself, the form element is the basic component of any form. Many times, forms are used to gather user feedback—personal information, opinions, or many other types of data. Using the form element—which consists of several input components like text fields, checkboxes, radio buttons, and submit buttons—an HTML form is generated. These components let users supply their information, therefore enabling their participation. Usually, forms are sent using the Hypertext Transfer Protocol (HTTP), which then sends the data to a server for handling. Either a GET or a POST request is used to pass over the data; the POST method is the most often used one for supplying sensitive or significant amounts of data.

It is not enough to just arrange form elements on separate pages if one wants forms that are user-friendly. One should give great thought to usability, accessibility, and efficacy, among other things. A well-considered form will guide the user through the data-entering process so that they may rapidly input the necessary information and submit it without becoming confused or annoyed. A good user experience results from the proper placement of form fields, the use of concise and clear labeling, and the inclusion of useful instructions or recommendations. Furthermore, forms should be responsive—that is, they should operate without any issues across a variety of devices and screen sizes. A responsive form is one that can be fit to several layouts and input techniques. This guarantees that the user, whatever their device— desktop computer, tablet, or mobile—can readily engage with the form.

Regarding the development of forms, usefulness is not the only consideration; another is accessibility. Online accessibility is in charge of making sure every user—including those with disabilities—can access and interact with content on the web. One instance of this is the provision of substitute ways of interacting with forms, such as keyboard navigation or screen audiences. For instance, forms should be suitably labeled using the label element, which links a text label with an input field. This is a vital capability since the screen reader will read aloud the label related to every form field. Moreover, the introduction of semantic HTML elements can improve the accessibility of forms by aggregating fields associated with one another and, therefore, provide context for users.

Working with forms and including user input depends mostly on the validation of the data process. Data validation guarantees that the material entered via a form is correct, complete, and displayed in a suitable structure. Validation can occur on the server side (on the server) as well as on the client side—in the browser. Because

JavaScript lets developers check the input before it is sent to the server handling it, it is often used for client-side validation. This gives users quick feedback that helps them to fix mistakes in real time. Common sorts of client-side validation include, for instance, looking for empty fields, making sure a valid email address is entered, and confirming that passwords fit specific criteria (like minimum length or complexity).

Client-side validation helps to improve the user experience since it reduces the likelihood that users will submit forms, including data that is either incomplete or erroneous. Still, it's important to remember that client-side validation is not totally perfect. JavaScript shouldn't be the only way to check security, as some browsers let it be disabled. Particularly important for sensitive data such as login passwords, payment information, and personal details; this ensures that only real and safe data is accepted. For these kinds of data, it is especially crucial.

Another crucial ability for working with forms is still the administration of form submissions. The data is sent to a server whenever a user files a form so it may be handled. The server runs the data in line with the request method—be it GET or POST—and then generates the pertinent answer. Should the submission to the server be successful, the server could show a success message or send the user to a confirming page. Should the form's submission prove to be problematic, the server may send back an error message. This notice could point to mistakes in an input format or missing necessary fields. Developers must treat form submissions in a way that provides users with clear comments absolutely critically. This will help users to know whether any corrections are needed or whether the submission was successful.

Furthermore, essential for a great range of web applications and form submissions, especially related to dynamic or interactive websites. Modern web development handles many forms asynchronously using AJAX, sometimes known as Asynchronous JavaScript and XML. AJAX allows one to send data from a form without resorting to reloading the whole page. This allows visitors to complete forms and get responses without having their contact with the website disrupted, therefore producing a more flawless user experience. A user turning in a contact form would then be handled by the server, who would then respond, indicating whether or not the submission was successful. This would occur without the user needing to page back off. When real time feedback is needed—as in the case of live search suggestions, form validation, or dynamic content updates— AJAX is usually used.

Furthermore, important is considering file upload management in addition to form submission. Many forms ask users to upload files, which lets them access a range of materials, including papers, pictures, videos, and other kinds of resources. By means of the input type="file"> element supplied by HTML, users can choose files from their local device and upload them to the server. Regarding file uploads, one should give security and any file size constraints great consideration. Developers have an obligation to ensure that given files are validated in a suitable way by looking for allowed file types and sizes. Developers should also include steps to stop harmful data from being entered. These safeguards could be using techniques that allow for safe file uploading or virus scanning of data.

One of the most important considerations while handling forms and user data acceptance is security. Attacks of many more sorts can be conducted against forms including SQL injection, cross-site request forgery (CSRF), and cross-site scripting (XSS). In terms of user input management, developers have to follow the best security standards to protect themselves from such attacks. For instance, input data should be cleaned and verified to ensure it cannot be used for any evil intent. Input fields should be properly escaped to stop possibly dangerous codes from running in the browser. Sensitive data—including credit card information and passwords—should be encrypted before being sent across the network in order to stop illicit access.

Forms are typically used to gather user data; nevertheless, they can also be used to change or remove previously gathered data. Furthermore, developers should be sure users already have the necessary rights before changing specific data. Should a user lack the necessary rights, for example, they should not be able to delete the account of another user or change private data.

Regarding user comments, forms, and user input are also really crucial. Many websites and web apps gather user input using forms. Among the several forms used are contact forms, surveys, ratings, and reviews. By means of these forms, companies and organizations can better grasp the needs, preferences, and experiences of their consumers. Improving goods and services depends on the gathering of customer comments since it provides important information on both positive and negative consumer preferences. Feedback forms' design and usefulness are equally vital as those of any other type. Feedback forms should be easy for consumers to complete and provide a practical way to express their ideas.

The abundance of mobile communication devices has fundamentally changed the design and use of forms. Mobile users often interact with forms using touch screens; this presents a special set of problems in relation to the layout, input methods, and responsiveness of the mobile application. To ensure that consumers will have a simple time interacting with mobile devices, regardless of the screen size or the method of their input, forms for them must be optimized.

In essence, forms and user input are crucial elements of web development since they enable users to interact with websites and online applications by means of data communication and comment provision. Establishing a wonderful user experience mostly depends on design, functionality, and form validation in terms of architecture. This is so because they ensure that the acquired data is safe, correct, and handled in a suitable way. Regarding gathering and analyzing user data, forms are the main tool. This covers simple contact forms to complex multi-step procedures. A website or online application cannot be effective overall without developers fully understanding the many elements of form construction, validation, submission, and security. Good input handling and form design help the application or website to be successful generally. The methods and technology used to manage forms and user input will keep becoming more advanced as the web develops, therefore ensuring that web applications remain dynamic, interesting, and safe for people all over the world.

Working with CSS and Classes in JavaScript

One of the most important things to grasp for the creation of dynamic websites is working with CSS and JavaScript classes. Thanks to this idea, developers may today change the visual look of objects discovered on the internet using scripting. Standing for "Cascading Style Sheets," Cascading Style Sheets is in charge of handling components including color, typography, spacing, placement, and responsiveness. HTML manages elements as well. The CSS framework bears both responsibility for the layout and design of a page. Conversely, JavaScript is the programming language that might change in DOM-a representation of the structure of the webpage containing the elements and styles of those elements. One can modify the DOM using JavaScript. CSS and

JavaScript let developers design websites that are not just visually dynamic but also quite interactive and responsive to real time user activities. The fact that these websites might be created helps to enable this. This section offers a study of how JavaScript uses CSS and classes to change styles, apply dynamic behavior, and enhance the general user experience. The section especially addresses how dynamic behavior is accomplished with HTML and CSS.

JavaScript's interaction with CSS via the Document Object Model (DOM) allows developers to dynamically make changes to HTML components and the styles connected with them. One of the most important techniques available to carry out this control is adjusting the CSS classes that elements belong to, therefore influencing their look. Many different HTML components can be styled using CSS classes and a body of style guidelines. Various HTML components can be styled using these classes. JavaScript allows creators to dynamically alter a webpage's presentation depending on user activities such as clicking, moving the mouse, or form submission. One can accomplish this by including, removing, or alternating among these three forms.

Using a class in CSS lets developers apply the same styles to several components without repeating the same declarations. This increases efficiency and flexibility. A class is a technique whereby several style rules can be aggregated under a single identifier. Designing buttons, headlines, or visuals consistent across an entire homepage is achievable with a class, for instance. One can accomplish this with fairly little effort. An HTML element subjected to a class will inherit the styles connected with the class at the moment of application. Conversely, the usage of JavaScript allows developers to include dynamic behaviors improving the user interface and beyond static styling.

Working with CSS classes in JavaScript, one of the most often used techniques is class list property manipulation. This is accomplished by way of the classList attribute. This function, included in the Document Object Model (DOM), allows one to readily access and change the classes linked to an HTML element. On components without directly changing the className field, the add(), remove(), and toggle() methods of the class List object let developers add, remove, or toggle classes. The extra, deleted, and toggled classes help to make this feasible. Among the several practical tools the classList object offers, these ones are among the most valuable ones. This makes it especially useful for the construction of dynamic web components that react to input from several users. Hitting a button could, as a sample, send a JavaScript code, improving the look of a div by adding a given class and altering its background color, size, visibility, or any mix of these.

Among the several tools JavaScript offers is the ability to directly change the style attribute of an element. Included in this capability are both the class List property and this capacity. Using this feature allows developers to dynamically apply particular CSS guidelines to an element to provide the intended impact. The user can change the width, height, background color, and font size of the element among other aspects of settings. Though it allows developers exact control over particular styles, changing CSS classes is more efficient and flexible than this approach. Less efficient and less flexible than the other approach, this one is also less suitable. Apart from increasing the maintenance difficulty of the code, explicitly changing the style of an element can also complicate management since it combines behavior with display logic. This is the reason it goes against the ideas of division of responsibilities in web development.

Using CSS classes together with JavaScript has many major benefits, one of which is the capacity to create designs that are not only responsive but also interactive. Developers can find events, including mouse clicks, hover actions, or scrolling, and then change the CSS of elements to respond. This is one avenue. One programming language available is JavaScript. One example of what JavaScript may accomplish is adding a CSS class that uses a zoom effect upon the user hovering over an image. JavaScript also allows a button to change color when pressing it. As both of these cases show, JavaScript may be used in many different ways. By means of this type of interaction, one can create an interesting user experience. Furthermore, this kind of interaction helps the website to have a dynamic and flexible look.

JavaScript also lets one create animations and transitions, which could be achieved by adding or deleting CSS classes defining the effects of animation and transition. One can reach this aim using JavaScript, the computer language. When it comes to bringing seamless visual changes into products over the course of a longer time, animated transitions and animations are absolutely essential. This could be seen in the triggering of a JavaScript function upon a button click by a user. This would thus result in the development of a class in charge of starting an animation, such as the slow development of a hidden element or the gradual introduction of a panel. JavaScript animations let developers create aesthetically pleasing but also functionally engaging user interfaces when combined with CSS animations.

The capacity of JavaScript and CSS technologies to change classes depending on particular criteria is another strong skill of their interaction. This is only one of the above-described qualities. Leveraging the toggle() method—which is available via the classList property—developers can add or delete a class depending on whether or not a class is currently being used on an element. This ability exists whether or not the class is under use. This approach is extensively used for the development of interactive components—such as dropdown menus, modals, or collapsible sections—that require the generation of interactions. JavaScript lets a class shown on a menu or panel display flip whenever a user clicks a button or icon. This toggle might either make the class visible or invisible, depending on the state the class is in right now. This lets developers create more complex and varied interfaces for their programs. This is made possible since extra JavaScript code or complex conditional statements are not needed.

Moreover, the development of single-page applications (SPAs) and the application of dynamic content changes depends on the administration of CSS classes in JavaScript, therefore aggravating the damage. In single-page apps, sometimes referred to as SPAs, the page loads and dynamically loads and changes its content. This does away with the requirement to reload the whole page. JavaScript is in charge of modifying the Document Object Model (DOM) and changing the styles in line with the modifications the user interacts with the program causes. For example, JavaScript allows the page to change its layout and look as a user moves between several views or components of the program. One can achieve this by either adding or deleting classes from several items. This guarantees that independent of the present level of the software, the user interface will keep giving the user a consistent and responsive experience.

JavaScript can be used to manage several classes at once in addition to adding and deleting single classes. Programmers may apply several classes to a single element by using the classList property. This helps them to attain more sophisticated styling and behavior in turn. For example, it is possible for a button to include an extra class that determines the hover effect in addition to a base class in charge of its look. Based on user interactions or other events, JavaScript allows one to dynamically create or delete these classes. One can work on this. This helps to build an extremely flexible and dynamic user interface with regard to its functionality.

Another crucial instrument for customizing the appearance of items on a webpage is the JavaScript use of CSS classes. JavaScript lets one use some classes designed to control object visibility, positioning, or presentation. One can utilize these classes to turn on or off material display ability. Showing a menu when a button is clicked or a loading spinner while content is being loaded asynchronously are two instances of when this is extensively employed. Both of these circumstances are ones in which, based on user input, material has to be revealed or hidden. These strategies help to improve the user experience and general quality of the experience by means of unambiguous visual signals and decreased demand for page reloads.

Often, using CSS classes for style modification is more effective than directly changing an element's style property. This is so because created CSS classes are This is so because CSS classes were created especially to address style modification. When the classList property is used to add, remove, or turn on classes, the browser can maximize the rendering time by recalculating styles and reflowing the layout only when it is absolutely required. This lets the browser greatly maximize the rendering process. This is of great relevance when it comes to programs that are needed to make constant modifications to the user interface since it guarantees that the website will remain responsive even in case of a notable volume of traffic. Furthermore, the use of classes to style ensures that the CSS is maintained apart from the JavaScript logic, therefore simplifying the maintenance and troubleshooting of the code.

One of the most important problems that arise when dealing with CSS and JavaScript classes is making sure the styles are used consistently across many browsers and applications. Among the most important difficulties that surface here is Every browser will show CSS styles in a somewhat different way; hence, some CSS attributes or classes cannot be supported by every browser. These are two realistic options. Usually, developers utilize JavaScript libraries (such as jQuery) or CSS preprocessors (like SASS or LESS) to guarantee consistent styling and to streamline the process of cross-browser compatibility. This is carried out in response to the provided difficulty. Furthermore, CSS frameworks like Foundation and Bootstrap offer pre-built classes fit for a broad spectrum of browsers. There are other ways one may apply these seminars. This allows developers to create responsive and well-designed layouts in a limited period of time without having to code their own CSS.

JavaScript could also be combined with CSS variables; a strong capability of CSS that lets values be reused all across a stylesheet. JavaScript allows one to combine with CSS variables. JavaScript can also be used in some circumstances besides CSS variables. One can put CSS variables in the stylesheet and then apply JavaScript to dynamically alter those variables. This condition makes it possible to create scalable and flexible styling that fits both adaptabilities. A developer creating a CSS variable for the main color of a website and subsequently utilizing JavaScript to dynamically change the value of that variable depending on user or system preference would demonstrate this. One could consider this to be a dynamic transformation. By applying this approach, one may easily change and theme a website as well as create more fluid transitions between the several design possibilities currently accessible.

Using CSS and classes in JavaScript clearly separates interests and is one of the most obvious advantages of these two languages. Among the benefits most clearly visible is this one. Using JavaScript for behavior and CSS for styling helps developers preserve modularity and code organization. These two languages taken together make this conceivable. Maintaining and updating both the functional and aesthetic features of a website is considerably easier when these two independent elements are considered. Making adjustments to either component of the website is much less difficult as styling is contained inside CSS classes and JavaScript manages functionality, avoiding any conflicts or misunderstandings. This division increases reusability since CSS classes and JavaScript functions can be used for a range of components or pages without the need to replicate the same code.

Ultimately, the construction of contemporary websites absolutely depends on the capacity to handle CSS and classes produced by JavaScript. Those who have this capacity can create interactive and responsive websites in addition to aesthetically pleasing ones. By changing the Document Object Model (DOM) and applying JavaScript CSS classes, developers may create interactive and responsive user input in real time user interfaces. The DOM can be changed, so this is made feasible. Design animations, transitions, and interactive components that help to improve the user experience generally by means of this dynamic approach to styling. These characteristics help the user experience to be improved generally. One must be able to change CSS and JavaScript classes if one is to create modern web programs that are not only aesthetically beautiful but also rather functional. Apart from the basic hover effects generation, this feature can also be used for the building of more complex apps with single-page characters. Producing aesthetically pleasing and interactive web experiences still depends mostly on an awareness of the interactions between JavaScript and CSS. This is so because the fast-advancing field of web development is still one.

CHAPTER IV

JavaScript in Action – Building Interactive Features

Dynamic Content Creation

In the field of contemporary web development, the creation of dynamic content is a necessary element that significantly influences the building of interactive and interesting user experiences. This entails the development of material capable of real time updates. Originally the norm for web pages, static content was replaced with dynamic content—which is meant to be adaptable to consumer needs and preferences. The constant evolution of the internet has brought forth this transformation in response to that advancement. These developments in web technologies—most especially JavaScript, HTML5, CSS3, and server-side programming languages—have made this shift possible. These developments make it possible to offer materials more interactive, customized, and flexible. Dynamic content—that is, anything on the internet either automatically updated or changed—or that is specifically created depending on user interaction—offers a more immersive and personalized experience. Any material of either of these two forms is referred to as "dynamic content."

The growing need for material that is both more interactive and more customized is one of the main forces behind the move toward dynamic content. Early on in the history of the internet, websites were simply digital pamphlets. These were stationary pages with material that was not susceptible to alteration or updating. It was challenging to distinguish between users depending on their preferences or behaviors, as these stationary pages presented the same information to every single visitor. The fast evolution of web technologies made it quite clear that a more dynamic approach was absolutely necessary. By means of dynamic content, one can create web pages that can be altered in real time depending on a variety of criteria, including user activity, location, or even the time of day. Dynamic content helps to make this feasible. Thanks to this evolution, web browsing is now far more fascinating. These days, users can find websites that react to their comments and generate tailored experiences. For users, this has greatly made online browsing far more appealing.

Executed inside the browser, the JavaScript programming language allows developers to make real time modifications to the architecture and look of web pages. As such, it is among the most useful instruments for producing works of material with dynamic components. Dynamic effects such as sliding menus, graphic carousels, real time data updates, and interactive forms can be created with JavaScript. Using JavaScript helps one produce these effects. Based on user activities, JavaScript allows developers to dynamically add, delete, or update elements on a website. Engaging with the software framework, Document Object Model (DOM), is the way this is accomplished. This makes it now feasible to create more interactive web pages. Simple animations to sophisticated applications under data control can all be found on these websites. Both kinds of websites are nowadays feasible.

A vital part of dynamic user interfaces, JavaScript is also necessary for the asynchronous loading of the content process. This is so because the process makes use of JavaScript, among other components. Every time a user engaged with a traditional website; the whole page had to be reloaded. This produced often irritating experiences in addition to slow ones. This means that site developers can load fresh material without reloading the whole page nowadays. This is enabled by the release of AJAX, an acronym for Asynchronous JavaScript and XML. This technique allows one to dynamically incorporate data retrieved from the server in the background into the website. The application of this technology helps to make this feasible. User experiences born from this are faster and more seamless. This is so because altering the entire page is not what is being done; the only item being changed is the one needed.

The use of server-side programming languages is an additional very vital element of creating dynamic content. Among these languages, PHP, Python, Ruby, and Node.js are some instances. On the server, these programming languages are applied to create dynamic websites. This occurs prior to the content being delivered to the user's browser. Server-side languages enable websites to access and evaluate database data. This information can thus be used by websites to create dynamic content especially for the user who is accessing them. Based on the consumer's browsing behavior or past purchases, for example, an online retailer may present a range of products for the user to choose from. Along the same line, a news website might show the user a different set of headlines based on their location or the subjects of their interest in reading about. Websites may create custom, data-driven experiences with a degree of sophistication far higher than what can be achieved with fixed pages thanks to server-side technologies. The previously listed technologies can create these experiences.

One of the most essential of the several major advantages this kind of material presents is the possibility to provide consumers with tailored experiences based on their particular demands. The fact that consumers are growing more and more used to the concept that websites will fit their own tastes and needs has made individualism a necessary element of modern web design. Dynamic content helps a website to react to users depending on their activities, preferences, and interactions with the site. If the user's browsing history or purchase behavior is taken into account, for instance, customized product recommendations might show on an online retailer. This would be the situation should the website consider user choices. Along the same lines, a social networking site might show posts from friends and groups a user engages with most often. This degree of customizing results in an experience that is more interesting for the users since it gives the impression that the website is catered to the particular interests of the visitors.

Furthermore, the process of creating real time data changes calls for the necessary component to be dynamic content. Live sports scores, stock market updates, and weather forecasts are among the dynamically changing sorts of material updated depending on real time data. These are several types of news and information. Two other instances are forecasts of the weather and stock market updates. JavaScript and AJAX enable websites to obtain this data from outside sources and change the page without a full page reload. The application of these technologies makes this feasible. This guarantees consumers of having access to the most recent information, which is vital in many different sectors including the entertainment sector, the media, and the financial sector, among others. Real time material is also used in interactive applications such as online games, chat systems, and tools for teamwork, therefore aggravating the damage. To interact with these applications, users must be able to view rapid updates depending on the activities of other users.

Apart from the personalizing and real time data that dynamic content providers, it helps to improve user experience by means of interactive components and thereby influences. Dynamic content helps one to do this. Forms on websites, for example, can dynamically validate user input in real time, therefore allowing them to offer a rapid response to the user without their having to submit the form. Furthermore, possible are the creation of intricate web apps featuring dynamic content. Customer portals, dashboards, and social networking sites are a few of these applications—all of which call for real time information and interactions.

Dynamic content creation is linked with certain difficulties, even if it has a lot of benefits. Performance obligations are one of the most important problems. Dynamic content is mostly dependent on JavaScript and server-side processing, both of which have the potential to cause performance bottlenecks should they not be done properly. These two technologies are really important for us. Should a website run too much JavaScript in the browser or make too many calls to the server, for example, the page will load slowly, and the user will have a bad experience. This can also result in the website loading more slowly. As such, maximizing the performance of dynamic content is of great relevance. Some of the ways in which this can be achieved are by using techniques that include lazy loading, caching, and cutting the JavaScript and CSS load requirements.

Ensuring that every browser is compatible with one another presents still another obstacle to be overcome. JavaScript is widely used to create dynamic content; hence developers must make sure their code runs across several browsers and devices in the same way. The developers are in charge of this. Differing browsers provide differing degrees of JavaScript and other web technologies' support; hence this will probably be a difficult task to complete. Tools like polyfills and JavaScript frameworks like jQuery can be quite helpful in helping one to relax these concerns. This is so because these instruments offer functionality that is uniform across browsers. To ensure that their websites operate as expected for all users, developers are nevertheless obliged to be aware of the possibility of compatibility problems and to rigorously test them on theirs.

Working with dynamic content calls for careful consideration of many crucial elements, one of which is security. Two kinds of attacks that can be used against dynamic websites are SQL injection and cross-site scripting (XSS). This is so because dynamic websites frequently rely on user input and activities. The responsibility of making sure all user input is correctly checked and cleaned rests with the developers. This is so because the developers have a duty to stop harmful codes from running on the website. Moreover, dynamic websites usually depend on databases to save and access data, so developers have to put security policies in place to prevent illegal access and data leaks. This is so since dynamic websites mostly depend on databases.

Another major factor should be optimization for search engines, sometimes referred to as SEO. Usually responsible for crawling static content, conventional search engines may occasionally cause problems in becoming indexed on the correct level depending on the type of content. Websites with dynamic content may also suffer sometimes. Over the past few years, this improvement has particularly been really clear. Dynamic material created on the server thanks to server-side rendering (SSR) technology can then be provided to the user as stationary HTML codes. This simplified procedure helps search engines crawl and index the data more easily. Pre-rendering can be seen in the creation of stationary HTML for dynamic pages ahead and delivery to search engines. Furthermore, helping to improve search engine optimization is this kind of pre-rendering. Developers must consider search engine optimization (SEO) even as they produce dynamic content. This is essential to guarantee that consumers may access their websites and that search engines may find them.

One can modify the structure, design, and functionality of a website to fit the device the user is using to access it. Dynamic content helps to make this feasible. On a desktop computer, for instance, a website may show graphics much smaller than on a mobile device or visuals far larger than they should be. Along the same lines, dynamic content can change the organizational structure of a website to make it more user-friendly on smaller screens, thereby enhancing the whole user experience. This is achieved by increasing the fit of the website for smaller screens.

Apart from user expectations, the future of dynamic content generation and the expansion of web technology are closely related. The two are tightly linked. As websites keep becoming more interactive and customized, it is projected that there will be an always growing demand for dynamic content. Rising technologies like WebAssembly and progressive web applications (PWAs) should significantly enhance the performance and capabilities of dynamic webpages. These technologies will enable consumers to have experiences that are much more complex and interesting. The process of creating websites will enable them to provide even more customized and adaptable material considering the particular behaviors and preferences of visitors. AI and ML will enable this by being included in the application development process.

One could argue that the development of contemporary websites depends critically on the creation of dynamic content. This form of content creation gives consumers experiences unique and interesting as well as interactive ones. Using server-side programming languages, JavaScript, and various other web technologies lets developers create websites able to react to user interaction, provide real time data updates, and provide individualized experiences. Developers can create these sites. Dynamic content can, however, lead to a lot of issues, including security and speed concerns, browser compatibility, and search engine optimization. As the technology supporting the web develops, dynamic content should become an ever more crucial part of the user experience. This will make it possible to create very interactive, immersive, and sophisticated websites.

Introduction to APIs and Fetch

Modern software development mostly depends on application programming interfaces, commonly known as APIs, in particular spheres. Thanks to this, different systems can interact with one another. Growingly important as software designs have evolved, application programming interfaces (APIs) enable a wide range of platforms, services, and apps to interact with one another as well as to exchange data, integrate data, and link with one another. Bridges between several software applications and application programming interfaces—also referred to as APIs—ensure that several programs may interact without running across any problems. One of the most basic languages employed to communicate with web application programming interfaces (APIs), which have grown in significance over the past few years for the reason of offering dynamic, interactive, and responsive webpages, is Among the languages used in connection with APIs is JavaScript. This is so given the Fetch API is among the most often used methods. A potent and innovative tool enabling users to quickly control the results and create asynchronous searches is the application programming interface (API). Those who wish to create strong, data-driven apps and services have to be completely aware of application programming interfaces (APIs) and how they work, as well as the part the Fetch API performs in linking with APIs. Those who want to create such applications and services must first meet this basic need.

A historic event in the annals of software development was the arrival of application programming interfaces (APIs). This event fundamentally changed the way applications interact with each other and exchange data. Applications were kept unique from one another and have limited means of communication with one another throughout history. This isolation led to the development of heavy-duty and repetitious systems. Software developers were driven to create every new application capability equal in nature. This led to the creation of repetitious and unwieldy systems. Often referred to as APIs, application programming interfaces were developed to solve this issue. Their providing of a uniform way for programs to interact with one another eliminates the need for the applications to have a knowledge of the inner workings of the other application. Applying programming interfaces (APIs) allows developers to access particular data or capabilities of an outside service or application. This thus helps their software development to be more modular, reusable, and effective.

Among the several powers application programming interfaces (APIs) offer are those related to data access from a database, data transit to a server, and even calls for particular services. APIs can help to enable a great spectrum of activities. Web application programming interfaces, quite widely used in the field of web development, enable communication across the internet. Often used by these application programming interfaces (APIs), the HyperText Transfer Protocol (HTTP) forms the basis on which the World Wide Web is built. This makes it possible to get access to them by simple searches that might be managed online. When a client wishes to access data or services provided by a server, an application programming interface (API) endpoint can get an HTTP request from the client—that of a web browser. The server will then either supply the requested data or a confirmation proving the success of the sought-after activity.

This makes it possible for developers to obtain data from outside sources without blocking the user interface, therefore avoiding this. Using Promises, a JavaScript tool that allows one to manage asynchronous actions in a way that is both more ordered and more efficient, Fetch stands out among its successors in one of its most important benefits. Promises—which represent a value either now or in the future—allow developers to manage asynchronous programming in a way that is more understandable and under control. Promises let us do this. Fetch helps developers run queries to the network, manage the answers to those requests, and undertake asynchronous data processing. This means they are free from worrying about the complexity and suffering related to callbacks, which are connected with past systems.

Working with application programming interfaces (APIs), developers often utilize the GET method to obtain data, the POST method to provide data, and the PUT or DELETE method to either alter or delete data. These techniques are applied in turn to acquire, present, and modify data. These techniques define the kind of interaction the client is seeking from the server; they are, therefore, part of the Hypertext Transfer Protocol (HTTP). The Fetch API helps developers to easily provide the method, headers, and content of the request since it makes the process of generating these inquiries rather simpler. The Fetch API's simplicity of the procedure helps to make this feasible. While they are making a GET call to an application programming interface (API), the Fetch API lets developers access data from a particular URL. The application then takes advantage of the gathered data. Fetch, an application programming interface (API), lets developers send data to a server anytime they create a post-request action. Typically, depending on the application programming interface (API), this data can be sent as JSON, XML, or form data.

Those working with the Fetch API certainly must be completely aware of the asynchronous character of HTTP queries. A standard synchronous operation will cause a function to run from top to bottom, therefore stopping any further activities until the function has finished its job. This approach is not appropriate since waiting for a response while in the process of generating network searches has the possibility of making the whole application inaccessible. Unlike synchronous operations, which forbid this, asynchronous operations enable the application to keep running even while it is waiting for the response. Asynchronous programming—that is, the ability of other code to run while it waits for a response from the server—is included in the Fetch application programming interface (API). This is so because asynchronous programming makes other code possible to execute. Promises are used to help to accomplish these. Promises give the program the means to handle the response as soon as it becomes available without interfering with its ability to meet other obligations in the interim.

Using the Fetch API will help one to manage the data coming from an application programming interface (API), offering several ways that can be merged in chains. The then() method is used to indicate what should happen once the response has been gotten. This lets one specify what ought to happen. Once the Fetch request has been received, for instance, developers have the chance to handle the data by converting it into a format the application can utilize, say JSON. This lets the information be handled much more. Developers have the freedom to make use of the response data in a range of ways, including altering the user interface, starting fresh activities, or saving the data for later use once the processing of the response data ends. The catch() method is used to recover from any mistakes that might develop during the request processing while it is in progress. The catch() method, for example, will be used should the server fail to be accessed or provide an error status code. The situation will determine this. This will enable the developer to efficiently correct the error in a suitable manner—that is, by showing the user an error message.

The Fetch Application Programming Interface (API) is used in a broad spectrum of applications including the creation of network requests and response header changes used to offer metadata and information about the answer. Among the headers, some instances of the data that might be included are the type of content, the response's length, and cache instructions. Headers can also feature additional bits of data. Having access to these headers enables developers to make better informed judgments on the treatment of response data. This raises the probability these choices will be taken. The developer could decide to decompress the data before working on it. The developer might decide, for instance, if the response has a header stating the content is compressed. Furthermore, should the response be cached, the developer could choose not to make another request, so less work is done by the server.

Including outside data and services into a web application is among the most often used Fetch API purposes. Among the most often used methods in the API is this one. One can accomplish this by working with outside third-party supplied application programming interfaces (APIs). For example, a developer creating a weather application could use a third-party provided weather application programming interface (API) to get real time weather data grounded on the user's location. To handle transactions, for example, a developer may choose an application programming interface (API) for a payment gateway. In the same vein, they may use social media APIs to show user entries on their website. The Fetch API provides the interface over which the client may execute data searches to the API and handle the response, so smoothly integrating the external service into the programme. This happens in line with the previously mentioned circumstances.

While the Fetch API streamlines dealing with web APIs, developers must keep some key issues in mind even if it does so. Fundamental to the procedure are these factors. Error handling is a crucial element that has to be considered since network requests may fail for a variety of reasons, including the fact that a server is absent or that a timeout has happened. This application programming interface (API) presents a strong system of error control. This approach helps creators to spot issues and gently address them. They might retrain the request or show the user a warning, for instance. Furthermore, security is a crucial element that has to be given thought especially in relation to sensitive data. To limit the potential of data being intercepted, API inquiries must be made utilizing secured channels—like HTTPS. The developers have the obligation to ensure that this occurs. Furthermore, developers are supposed to follow the best standards for the security of API keys, tokens, and credentials before starting their employment. This is the situation when they are interacting with APIs needing authentication.

Furthermore, while working with APIs and Fetch, one should keep in mind how to effectively control cross-origin resource sharing—also known as CORS. Cross- Origin routing (CORS) is a security method used by browsers to stop rogue websites from requesting illegal access to other domains. This is undertaken to stop harmful websites from proliferating. The browser will impose Cors restrictions when a web application requests an API housed on another domain. This happens any moment the application calls. Developers must either create workarounds, such as the use of a server-side proxy or make sure the application programming interface (API) they are dealing with is compatible with CORS in order to get past these constraints. To break free from these limitations, both of these opportunities are required.

Apart from the performance aspects of CORS, developers also have to consider the consequences of several API inquiries. Retrieving data from outside APIs could cause delays in development. This is particularly crucial in situations when the server is located far away or when the network connection is really poor. Developers can help to minimize this by optimizing the quantity of API searches conducted, localized result caching to prevent repetitive calls, and pagination to access vast volumes of data in smaller chunks that are not only simpler to handle but also more manageable. Proper handling of API requests and answers by developers helps them to create web apps that effectively interact with services not included in their own architecture. This enables the developers to create effectively running web apps.

Its ability to simplify the construction of dynamic, interactive, data-driven online applications that are fundamental components of current web development has made it indispensable. This capacity has helped it to evolve generally into a necessary component. Developers who fully grasp application programming interfaces (APIs) and how to use the Fetch API will be able to include a great range of outside services in their products. This openness lets creators of more potent apps innovate with ease. These services can address a broad spectrum of subjects, from meteorological data to payment processing. Dealing with APIs and Fetch presents many challenges that have a bearing on each other. Among these difficulties include security, error management, and CORS. Still, these difficulties can be resolved with appropriate application design and best practices applied. The creation of intricate, real time online apps that give users experiences that are rich and interesting will depend much on application programming interfaces (APIs) and fetch.

Basic Project: Interactive Quiz App

By means of the production of a simple project, like an interactive quiz app, developing skills in programming and web development is not only advantageous but also fun. It offers the chance to bring these ideas to life, therefore enabling the application of fundamental ideas including variables, functions, control structures, and event handling—all of which are absolutely vital for JavaScript and web development generally. Apart from giving developers—especially those who are just starting out—the ability to get essential practical knowledge in the design of interactive applications, this project also gives them front-end programming experimentation opportunities. This is a great way to start with web development since developing an interface that appeals to users, getting input from users, and providing dynamic feedback depending on how users interact with the website takes the front stage. It is thus a great way to start with web programming.

An interactive quiz app will usually consist of a series of questions, each of which has more than one solution most of the time. At the end of the test, the application should give the user a final score, give quick comments on the correctness of their answers, and track user development all through the test. Beginning with the awareness of the needs and working through the stages of planning, coding, testing, and debugging, the project is developed in numerous phases. The interactive quiz app mostly aims to produce a responsive and fun user experience. This is achieved concurrently with a knowledge of the foundations of web development technologies, including HTML, CSS, and JavaScript.

Finding the main framework of an interactive quiz app comes first in order to start the designing process. The software must show a sequence of questions; the user must be provided multiple-choice responses for every question, and the application must also note user responses if it is to operate as intended. Every time a user interacts with the application; it will instantly give comments to them based on whether or not the responses they offer are true. Although this function is not required for the most basic versions of the smartphone application, the program must also have a timer to raise user involvement. Furthermore, it is rather crucial to have a score monitoring system so that the user may get knowledge about their own performance. Furthermore, improving the user experience is the possibility to go to different questions or retake the test.

Planning the structure of the application—which comprises both the user interface and the core functionality—comes next once the project's needs have been decided upon. This stage starts the moment the needs of the project are known. The user interface (UI) must be straightforward to traverse as well as uncomplicated, basic, and understandable. Apart from showing questions, another for offering responses—radio buttons or clickable choices—and still another for offering comments. The feedback section will review the user's answer to ascertain whether it is accurate or erroneous.

These elements will form the arrangement that will be employed. Two useful additions to the fundamental elements already in place may be a timer and a progress bar showing the remaining time or the user's quiz progress. These components would help to add something. Maintaining a record of the selected responses, matching those answers to the ones that are accurate, and subsequently changing the score in line with the evaluation marks the most important action in guaranteeing that the application is running as intended. After that, the HTML file's structure is developed, therefore starting the process of development. HTML will help with the building of the static elements of the app, which consist, among other things the question section, response choices, and buttons. This will help the application to seem orderly and neat, free of any clutter. Furthermore, CSS will aid in the management of the spacing, fonts, colors, and other visual aspects of the app, so fostering an environment interesting for the user.

JavaScript is a major contributor to the interactive portion of the quiz app being much improved. JavaScript will be in charge of managing the functionality of the application once the program layout is finished. This covers user input recording, matching it with the right responses, score computation, and real time feedback provision, in addition to the feedback-giving technique. Using functions in sequence will help to regulate the flow of the experience on the test. Among these purposes will be the capacity to answer the next inquiry or expose the overall score. Furthermore used, is JavaScript to create dynamic changes to the page without requiring page refreshing. This helps the consumer to have a flawless experience.

Among the several basic features of an interactive quiz app, one of the most crucial is its capacity to recognize and react to user input. JavaScript will be used to control the alternatives the user chooses. This holds true whether the user is clicking on checkboxes, radio buttons, or any other item. Including event listeners into JavaScript's interactive components lets the programming language track and react to user activities including a click or a change. Once it has this knowledge, it can react in a suitable way. For instance, JavaScript will examine whether or not an answer a user chooses fits the right response and then change the score. Should the answer be accurate, the program might show a good message before tackling the next question. Should the user respond with a mistake, the application might show them an error notification and offer chances for the user to complete the task once more.

Engaging the users and getting their comments is another vital component of the project that has to be managed. After every question, the program ought to give the user comments on whether or not their answer was fitting. The program should produce this kind of comment. Either altering the response that has been chosen or displaying a notice next to the question indicating whether the response was accurate or false can help to accomplish this. These are both reasonable choices. Giving users fast comments helps them to improve the quality of their educational process. This is achieved by helping people to understand their mistakes and inspire suitable responses. Although this will depend on the level of difficulty the program presents, it is also likely that the response will offer hints or explanations.

Apart from the capacity to provide comments, the application has to be furnished with a rating system. The right responses given by the user are noted using a simple scoring system, which subsequently gives the user a total score at the test conclusion. Arriving at a score by adding one point to the total for every response that is accurate and complete is achievable. The score may also be calculated more complexly, with different points awarded for questions of differing degrees of difficulty. This would be a different approach to figure the score. The application then shows the user's overall score together with a message, like "Well Done" or "Try Again," based on the end result. This comes following the last stage of the application.

One of the most important features of interactive quiz applications is making sure users advance the quiz in a timely fashion. Either automatically going on to the next question or letting the user select a button to go, the program should let users advance through questions one at a time. These are both reasonable choices. JavaScript allows one to track the present question index and subsequently change the question shown in line with that index. One can engage in this. Once the test ends, the program shows the last result, thereby giving the user a chance to evaluate their general performance.

Apart from its main functions, the system could be improved with more complex features meant to raise the general quality of the user experience. For example, adding a timer to the question may give the whole experience an instantaneous quality. A countdown timer would start at the beginning of the quiz and cease either when the user completed it or when their allowed time ran out. After that, the program might send the user a message including the whole time spent finishing the test. This will further involve the user by making them successful, hence motivating them to keep using the program. Apart from this, one could consider including a progress indicator showing the percentage of the test that has been successfully finished. The visual depiction of their development helps the users to stay motivated to complete the quiz to a high degree.

Should the program allow a lot of rounds or categories of questions, users should be able to navigate between the several rounds or categories of questions. For example, the user may be able to play another quiz on another topic after finishing one on a particular one. This is only one instance. JavaScript allows one to show the questions in a dynamic form depending on the decisions the user takes; they can be arranged into categories.

Regarding the creation of an interactive quiz app, the procedure consists of multiple iterations of testing and improvement incorporated. It is the responsibility of the developers to guarantee that the application is free of any problems, that the user experience is continuous, and that the functionality operates in the way it was meant to. This phase lasts. Any problems that might arise—including but not limited to erroneous scores, buttons that do not work as expected, or the program that does not go to the next question—must be addressed right once. Apart from verifying that an application performs as expected during testing, it is also essential to make sure the software fits many devices and screen sizes. Adoption of responsive design techniques enables the changing of the layout and formatting of the question, therefore facilitating the necessary change to achieve the intended effect. This action will make the quiz easily available and used on several platforms.

Testing and debugging the application will comprise the next phase; program deployment will follow from this. Either hosting the quiz app on a server or using a tool like GitHub Pages will help you to enable anyone to view it. These are going to be required choices both of which This phase allows developers the choice to distribute their work to different people. This is carried out in order to get user comments, which is an essential element of the learning process. Attaching it to a personal website or distributing it on social media allows one to make the application accessible to a lot more people after it has been launched.

The developer might investigate the prospect of creating an interactive quiz app by adding more advanced features as they grow more experienced. Features that might fit this category include the ability to save user scores in a database, the supply of more challenging question kinds, or the inclusion of images and multimedia. Other possibilities that developers could consider include the integration of the program with other platforms, such as social media, for the aim of distributing findings or the addition of the possibility of following a user's development over time. Both of these choices are instances of other choices. These elements not only make the program more advanced but also more practical and raise the possibility of users helping the product to be developed.

In essence, creating a simple interactive quiz app is a great way for developers—especially beginners—to practice and become experts in fundamental web development subjects such as JavaScript, HTML, and CSS. Software engineers, in particular, should find this extremely true. Especially accurate for people just beginning their careers. Building this application provides developers with chances to learn user input management, feedback presentation, quiz flow control, and integration of advanced features, including timers and progress indicators. This speaks to the evolution of the application. Before working on more complex web projects, the quiz app allows developers to hone basic skills and test fresh ideas. It achieves this by giving more challenging web applications a strong basis for growth. If the developers keep honing and extending the project, they could increase their talents and gain a more thorough awareness of how to create dynamic and interactive web apps.

Debugging and Browser Tools

Debugging is one of the most crucial components of software development; this is especially relevant in the field of web development, where the complexity of applications has greatly grown. It is absolutely vital to be able to find, diagnose, and fix problems in a timely manner if we are to offer reliable web apps since it will help us to create such applications. More recent browsers have included robust development tools to make this process simpler. Using these tools, developers have the chance to examine, check, and fix their code from inside the browser. These tools have become an integral part of a developer's toolkit since they provide a wide spectrum of capabilities that simplify debugging and increase productivity.

More often known as DevTools, the browser developer tools are included in all of the main web browsers—including Google Chrome, Mozilla Firefox, Microsoft Edge, Safari, and Opera. Every one of these top web browsers includes these tools. Apart from a broad spectrum of other activities, this set of tools provides developers with a suite of tools enabling them to review HTML and CSS, debug JavaScript, monitor network traffic, analyze performance, and carry out other diverse tasks. By means of DevTool, developers may make educated decisions and promptly address any issues that might surface throughout the course of the project. Realizing this goal depends on offering real time analysis of the activity of web apps.

Many important capabilities are included in tools for browser development. Examining and modifying the Document Object Model (DOM) and Cascading Style Sheets (CSS) of a webpage is one of these features. When developers utilize this capability, they may review the structure of their HTML, evaluate styles that have been applied, and make temporary changes in order to test improvements without having to edit the source code. When it comes to fixing problems with the layout, responsive testing designs, and on-demand style adjustments experimentation, tools like these are very vital.

Another absolutely vital technique used by browser developers is JavaScript debugging. These tools let browser developers build webpages. By means of the JavaScript console, developers can run code snippets, study error messages, and record outputs for analysis. The JavaScript console grants these features. Thanks to the Sources panel—which in some browsers is also known as the Debugger— developers can also set breakpoints, walk through code line by line, and inspect the call stack and variable values at each execution step. Developers can possess both of these skills. These traits help one to uncover logical errors or unexpected behavior in scripts and simplify the acquisition of a more thorough awareness of the flow of code execution. It also makes it simpler to spot scripts that act in odd directions.

Network monitoring is a necessary element in debugging web applications. This is particularly true for apps, which mostly depend on asynchronous data fetching and API interactions. By means of the Network panel provided in DevTools, developers can review all the network requests made by the program. With this panel, developers may monitor the payloads, response times, and status codes linked with every request. Solving problems related to data retrieval requires this knowledge, which is, therefore, absolutely essential. Among these issues are those involving unsuccessful queries, sluggish answers, and erroneous data formats.

By means of performance analysis tools included in browser developer tools, one can grasp the behavior of web programs under operation. By means of performance profiles, developers can spot memory leaks, waste of code routes, and bottlenecks. Documenting and evaluating the performance profiles will help one do this. First of all, knowing how resources are used and the sites of delays helps software developers improve the responsiveness of their apps and the general user interface. This will help them to raise the general user experience.

Tools for browser developers offer features designed especially to fit the needs of individual development projects. These aspects complement the main purposes of these tools, which usually include, for example, among other storage options, cookies, local storage, and session storage, the Application panel in Chrome DevTools gives developers the means to study and change several storage techniques. Debugging issues connected to user sessions, preferences, and authentication tokens is one especially useful application of this capability.

Modern DevTools also features accessibility inspection tools, which let developers assess and enhance the accessibility of their online apps. These tools highlight the elements with accessibility concerns—such as missing ARIA traits or inadequate color contrast—and provide choices for fixing these problems. These instruments guarantee the addressing of accessibility problems. Many countries have legal requirements for maintaining accessibility; hence, these technologies are not only advised but also quite important for guaranteeing compliance and promoting diversity. This is so because, not only is accessibility a suggested practice but also a legal requirement.

Device emulation features of browser development tools enable one of the means by which responsive design testing is facilitated. To examine how their applications look visually across several devices, developers can replicate many screen sizes, resolutions, and orientations of devices. This lets programmers see how their apps look on several devices. This capability is absolutely essential for building web designs that are responsive and mobile-friendly, and that can support a great range of users.

Still, another area that would profit from the help browser developer tools offer is security. One can learn about the present situation of security on a webpage by means of the Security Panel. These revelations address HTTPS certificates, mixed content warnings, and several other possible hazards. Should developers spot and resolve any possible security issues early on in the development process, they will be able to safeguard user information and guarantee that consumers still trust their products.

The development of browser developer tools has been motivated by a rising degree of sophistication in debugging capabilities. The production of these instruments has been inspired by this need. The foundation for integrated development tools was much shaped by early development tools including Firebug for Firefox. These tools provide real time HTML and CSS editing, JavaScript debugging, and network monitoring, among other uses. The growing complexity of online applications has driven browser manufacturers to expand and enhance their development tools to satisfy ever rising needs of developers. This is in reaction to the growing sophistication of online apps.

For example, Chrome DevTools has made more advanced tools—like Lighthouse, which can assess web app performance—available along with accessibility and search engine optimization. Analogous in nature, Microsoft Edge DevTools, built on the Chromium engine, provides features akin to those of other tools while also adding extra elements to Microsoft services. These developments are a mirror of the continuous dedication to provide developers with complete tools for the creation of highly quality web apps.

Successful debugging in practice requires the use of several tools and a mix of several approach tactics. Usually starting with consistent reproduction of the problem, developers may have to configure particular settings or use several inputs. They start with this first action. Once they have proved that the problem can be replicated, they can use breakpoints and step-through debugging to track the path the program takes when running and investigate the states of the variables. One of the several benefits of logging messages to the console is that it might reveal information on program activity at several phases.

One tool that lets developers share debugging sessions or export diagnostic data is facilitating cooperative debugging. This function also facilitates team working for developers. Playwright, among other tools, makes it simple to automate testing and debugging across a variety of browsers and devices. For example, Chrome DevTools allows one to record and share performance profiles by means of its utilization. These characteristics are quite beneficial in situations involving teams, where a lot of developers are needed to collaborate to solve challenging problems since they enable several developers to work together.

Including browser developer tools in the development process has the possibility to increase the quality of the code as well as the output of the process. These instruments give rapid feedback and the ability to evaluate changes in real time, therefore reducing the time that passes between problem detection and their resolution. When followed, this iterative process supports agile development approaches and continuous integration practices. These methods are rather common in situations when frequent deployments and short development cycles are the norm.

Moreover, it is impossible to stress in any one direction, form, or shape the educational value of browser developer tools. Novice developers who utilize these tools have a hands-on learning environment where they may play with code, see changes' impacts, and gain a better knowledge of web technologies. Other materials abound that improve knowledge and skill development. These materials come from browser companies and comprise tutorials and documentation.

In essence, the use of development tools for browsers and software for debugging defines one of the most significant features of modern web development. They deliver to developers' capacity in speedy discovery and resolution of problems, performance optimization, assurance of security and accessibility, and high-quality user experiences. As the technology behind the web keeps developing, these tools will always be essential. This is so because they enable developers to produce the future generation of internet programs by handling fresh issues and making them realistic.

CHAPTER V

The Future of JavaScript and Next Steps

Modern JavaScript Features (ES6+)

The method of creating web apps has completely changed since contemporary JavaScript capabilities—which were first introduced with ES6 (ECMAScript 2015) and extended through later versions like ES7, ES8, and many more—were included in the play. These characteristics have helped to bring about this metamorphosis. These characteristics have helped JavaScript to expand its possibilities, thereby increasing its power, lowering its complexity of use, and enabling its fulfillment of the criteria of contemporary development methods. From its early days, when it was routinely attacked for its quirks and limitations, to the present, when JavaScript is a strong, fully functional programming language, modern characteristics have been a major factor in its development. This has been the case from the time it was initially presented until right now. One important element in enabling this development all around has been the inclusion of modern traits. The several enhancements ES6 brought about by itself greatly enhanced the syntax, readability, and utility of the language. The several changes in this regard reflect JavaScript has come a long way in terms of its ability to complete previously challenging jobs once newer ECMAScript versions were published. These most recent models have brought features even more sophisticated than those of the previous iterations.

Two of the fundamental characteristics that ES6 brought in let and const are those that enable the introduction of several other basic features. These keywords enable block level scope, which is a major technological advance over the var keyword, which was formerly used for variable declarations. Variables were declared with the var keyword in essence. Var had function scope since variables could be retrieved anywhere, they were defined throughout the course of the function. Variables might thus be accessed at any point during the function. This often resulted in behavior that surprised me, especially when working in loops or conditions. Particularly, this was true. Conversely, let and const allow one to limit the range of variables to the block indicated. One achieves this by combining the two. This helps to eradicate a lot of issues and defects usually seen in the building sector. Variables come in two flavors: let and const. Whereas const is used for variables whose values should not be reassociated, let is used for variables whose values should not be reassigned. This guarantees that particular values' immutability—that they cannot be altered—may be confirmed. This improvement made the code less prone to mistakes and more consistent, therefore improving the general experience for developers. Thus, the whole experience was much improved.

One more notable addition by ES6 from previous versions is the syntax for arrow functions. Particularly for relatively short anonymous functions, the use of arrow functions helps to create functions in a more condensed form. The arrow syntax not only cuts the phrase short but also changes the behavior of this keyword. This is thus because the arrow syntax performs actions differently from others. The context in which the function is called dynamically defines its value in the traditional sense. This context shapes this value. The setting in which this value functions determines its basis. This usually results in problems when working with callbacks or event handlers. This phenomenon is especially troubling. Conversely, arrow functions lexically bind this, therefore carrying with them from the scope around them the value of this. Mathematical functions of the kind arrow functions are those ones This simplifies the handling of passed-along functions as arguments and helps to lower the often-occurring error count. In increasingly complex codebases especially, it helps since it simplifies the maintenance of this.

ES6 also brought template literals, which helped JavaScript's string management to be much improved. Template literals helped to bring forth this improvement. Using the plus operator was essential to concatenating strings before ES6, and typically, this produced code that was harder to understand. It was particularly true in cases when variables or expressions were included in strings. One can streamline the string interpolation process by using template literals, which are included in backticks (). Applying the $ { } $ operator allows one to directly embed expressions inside a string, hence supporting this functionality. This results in significantly simpler string manipulation, which is especially helpful when working with complicated strings or producing dynamic content. Writing code that is both clear and succinct benefits much from template literals. This is so because they can manage multi-line strings—previously challenging to control with JavaScript. Given this capacity, template literals are quite useful.

With the release of ES6, a major technological development, another striking ability—destructuring—

was added. Destructuring lets one extract values from arrays or objects and then store those values in unique variables apart from one another. This feature is really helpful, especially when dealing with complex data structures or when handling functions returning a lot of results. Developers used to access array members or object characteristics individually before the concept of destructive was developed. Code produced as a result could be repetitious and overly complicated. This practice was stopped once destructuring was applied. By means of destructuring, developers can directly assign a great number of values to variables in a way that is both more compact and logical than the traditional programming approaches. Especially helpful when working with intricate data structures, this function simplifies the code and improves its maintainability.

Destroying and the spread and rest operators both employ the same syntax, so their links are really strong. These two guys work for the same company. One can retrieve elements from arrays or properties from objects by means of the spread operator. One can use this to merge arrays, clone objects, or provide parameters into functions. This helps one to finish these chores more easily. To compile a set of values into an array, the remainder operator is used in the same way as before. This is a very useful method for building functions that can accept a changing number of parameters. Since they help to provide increased language flexibility, both the spread operator and the rest operator are valuable in JavaScript writing. This adaptability helps one to have a syntax that is not only more expressive but also more succinct within the framework of working with arrays and objects.

Classes were also included in ES6, which brought object-oriented programming (OOP) ideas to JavaScript in a way the user would find more ordered and familiar. Classes also originated with ES6. Before ES6, prototypes constituted the basis for object creation and inheritance in JavaScript; this made management and understanding challenging. For engineers who had lately worked with other object-oriented programming languages, this was especially true. Defining objects, creating constructors, and establishing inheritance became significantly less difficult once class syntax was adopted. This was a considerable development. Though the class terminology still derives from JavaScript's prototype-based inheritance model, the class system offers a more user-friendly and straightforward interface for working with objects and their attributes. This is so because the class system is based on the idea of categories. JavaScript grew more friendly for developers who were already familiar with class-based languages like Java or C++ due to this inclination toward more ordered object development. This came about from the move toward more under control object creation.

Moreover, a major development was ES6, the variant of the language that adopted modules. Before the release of ES6, developers had to rely on outside libraries or complex patterns such as Immediately Invoked Function Expressions (IIFEs) if they were to attain modularity in JavaScript. This was so because, at the time, JavaScript lacked a native module system. The creation of modules allowed programmers to divide their code into more doable portions that might be recycled. This makes organizing thorough codebases far simpler for programmers. Using modules lets one export objects, variables, or functions from one file and subsequently import them into another program. This capability helps modules to encourage better code organization and the division of tasks as well as responsibility. The module architecture also helps developers test and debug their apps since they may segregate functionality in different files and import just the necessary components into every area of their program. This is so since the module structure lets developers import just the most important parts. This modular method has evolved into a necessary part of modern JavaScript programmer development due to the spread of frameworks and build tools depending on modular code. Given the reliance of modular code on frameworks, this is especially true.

Following the significant progress made with the introduction of Promises in ES6, the conventional callback-based method of asynchronous programming has been much improved. This is a notable development. Before Promises came out, JavaScript's asynchronous code management usually required the usage of highly nested callback techniques. Promises changed all of that, but what was usually referred to as "callback hell." Promises offer a simpler, more orderly way to read into the management of asynchronous actions—that is, network requests or file operations. A Promise is a representation of the ultimate success or failure of the activity, therefore depicting an asynchronous operation. It also allows one to initiate a chain reaction of the next events following the completion of the operation. This results in far less asynchronous code flow, which not only increases its readability but also facilitates maintenance of it. Promises give a better ability to manage mistakes than callbacks. This is the reason the.catch() function allows mistakes to be consolidated, therefore helping to avoid them.

Incorporating the async and await keywords in later versions of the ECMAScript programming language was meant to increase asynchronous programming possibilities even more. Thanks to these keywords, developers can create asynchronous code in a way that seems more synchronous. One uses both of these keywords in concert with one another. Whenever at all feasible, these two keywords are often employed in concert with one another. This makes it reasonable to create asynchronous code in a more straightforward, understandable style. It also removes the requirement for complex chaining of then() and catch() techniques, hence removing the demand for such chaining.

Furthermore, the debut of ES6 and later revisions brought about several minor improvements just as worthwhile. These enhancements were also introduced. By means of default parameters, it is possible to create default values for function parameters, therefore eliminating the need for human checks for unclear values. This makes hand checks obsolete. Known as Object.assign(), this approach enables combining objects or making shallow copies of objects simple. Many of the chores that are often connected to object management so become simpler. Originally designed to offer a more consistent means of NaN value detection, the Number.isNaN() method Its debut started with this main driving force. This was done to prevent the possibility as the usual NaN() approach yielded unexpected consequences.

The exponentiation operator (**) in ES7 helped to somewhat simplify the operation of increasing numbers to power. This was a notable development. This operator can be used in place of the more compact and user-friendly conventional Math.pow() function. Object.entries() and Object.values() are among ES8's several other useful tools for working with object attributes that simplify matters. Along with the advent of async/await, one of the features included was these ones. The ES9 version of JavaScript programming language was much improved with the inclusion of rest/spread characteristics for objects. These characteristics make it possible to regulate an object's features in a way that is both more effective and stronger.

Thanks to these additional characteristics, the contemporary JavaScript environment—which has evolved—has become a tool indispensable for developers working on a wide spectrum of online applications, ranging from simple webpages to many web apps with several facets. The development of the language, which has made it more flexible, strong, and expressive, allows developers to create more complex and simpler to manage programs. This is thus because the language has evolved into a more extendable, strong, and expressive tool. As JavaScript advances with subsequent versions of ECMAScript, we may expect even more modifications that would further enhance the development experience and help to meet the criteria of a technical landscape always changing. These developments enable us to satisfy the criteria of a technologically changing environment. JavaScript has become somewhat well-known as one of the most often used programming languages in the world today because of the developments brought about by ES6 and the following versions. This results from ES6's bringing about these innovations.

JavaScript in the Modern Ecosystem

Originally used for the client side of the web application building, JavaScript is a computer language. Still, it has become among the most important technologies available for modern software development. Many things, including interactive web pages, mobile apps, and server-side apps, are built on it as their foundation. JavaScript has evolved over time to meet the needs of developers and companies striving toward the production of sophisticated, rich, and efficient user experiences. The web's expansion follows that pattern as it keeps changing toward more dynamism. JavaScript has evolved into the language of the modern web thanks in part to its involvement in the creation of interactive webpages as well as its inclusion into server-side architectures and mobile platforms. This has helped JavaScript's position as the language of the modern web to grow more solid.

Given the present environment, it is possible to follow JavaScript's evolution all the way back to its first creation. Originally meant to be a client-side scripting language used to change web pages as they were being viewed in a browser, JavaScript is a programming language. Its main purpose was to enable basic types of interaction, therefore facilitating one of their functions. Among these interactive forms were form validation, dynamic content modifications, and simple animations. Though at the time this could have seemed to be a quite small niche, the expansion of more sophisticated online applications and websites revealed the limitations of early JavaScript in a fairly short period of time. The developers were searching for more powerful technologies if they could produce more in-depth and sensitive user experiences. This resulted in the creation of JavaScript frameworks and libraries, which greatly improved the usability and value of the language for a broad spectrum of uses.

Asynchronous JavaScript and XML, or AJAX, is an abbreviation that marks the first major advancement in the field of web development. It made it possible for dynamic changes on web pages to be made without the whole page reconfiguration needed. This allowed developers to create more dynamic and responsive webpages, which finally helped to produce online apps functioning at a level more similar to that of desktop applications. This metamorphosis affected not just the expansion of the JavaScript programming language but also the complete growth of the web development ecosystem. Developer execution of JavaScript on the server was not available till lately. But Node.js opened the door for this to become feasible. Node.js was able to manage a great volume of concurrent connections in an effective way by using an architecture driven by events and devoid of blocking. This was made feasible by the fact that it did not block. By means of JavaScript implemented on the server side, developers were able to create full-stack apps utilizing a single language starting with the client and terminating with the server, therefore opening new opportunities. Node.js, which, together with the increasing need for real time applications, was the driving force behind the phenomena, explains JavaScript's explosive surge in popularity in environments outside of the browser.

Node.js, which was in charge of introducing the idea, also helped to highlight the "JavaScript runtime" in the business. Most people agreed that JavaScript was a language used just on the browser side before Node was launched. Servers, back-end logic processing, and even database transaction administration are being built using JavaScript right now. As JavaScript runtimes like Node.js proliferate, this is getting more and more common. This paradigm shifts greatly changed the field of web development. This change made it possible for JavaScript to manage the whole development stack—from front-end to rear-end components. JavaScript could thus run over the whole stack under supervision. Using the full-stack JavaScript development method resulted in a single development environment. This platform lets developers collaborate using the same language throughout the program life. This meant that the learning curve for developers who knew JavaScript already was much lowered, therefore streamlining the process of building contemporary online apps. For those coders, this proved to be really advantageous.

Many important elements have contributed to JavaScript code being contemporary. Among these elements is the expansion of JavaScript frameworks and libraries— React, Angular, and Vue.js, most especially. These libraries have been in charge of bringing about a radical change in front-end development since they offer original ways to build intricate user interfaces. Among the approaches falling under this category are declarative rendering, state management, and reusable components. Facebook developed React. This creative approach enhances the efficiency of online applications since it updates just the updated components of the Document Object Model (DOM), not creating the whole page once more. Google used a more opinionated approach when creating the web application Angular. It provides a complete solution for the construction of single-page applications (SPAs), which might be used to create apps that just need one page. Built-in dependency injection and two-way data binding help to achieve this. One solution that was not only flexible but also simple to understand came from the lightweight framework known as Vue.js. Its popularity grew in part from the ease with which it might be included in other projects.

By means of these frameworks, developers were given the means necessary to create not just highly interactive and performable apps but also ones with less code and a more simplified architecture. They were able to abstract away a good bit of the difficulties associated with adjusting the Document Object Model (DOM), controlling state, and handling asynchronous events. This allowed developers to focus less on daily chores and more on the construction of features. In the field of contemporary front-end development, these models still maintain a first place and their use is becoming more and more common lately. They thus have a great impact on the way in which developers interact with data on the web and design user interfaces.

Apart from its use in client-side systems, JavaScript has further proved its importance as a major element in modern web development by means of its involvement in the creation of mobile applications. This has strengthened JavaScript's importance even more. Thanks to the availability of technologies, including React Native, which is a framework established by Facebook, developers are now able to create native mobile applications for iOS and Android using JavaScript. Both iOS and Android smartphones could find use for these apps. React's declarative component model allows developers to create mobile apps with the same ideas they apply for online development. React Native helps to make this possible sense React uses this model. This revelation has made JavaScript an ability even more valuable than it was a few years back. Using their current knowledge of JavaScript, developers may now create cross-platform apps. This greatly reduces the time and effort required for the growth of initiatives.

Not limited to the React Native framework, another area of interest, JavaScript's impact on the mobile environment goes beyond. Two other technologies that have helped JavaScript's scope to be expanded are NativeScript, which lets Vue.js create native mobile apps, and Ionic, built on Angular. Two other technologies that have expanded JavaScript's reach are both of these ones. Web developers might so concentrate on creating mobile applications rather than others. JavaScript's use has grown recently as it can close the gap between online and mobile development, therefore enabling both. This is so because it enables developers to use web tools, enabling them to create native mobile apps.

This adaptability also extends to various industries, like desktop software development, game creation, and even Internet of Things (IoT)-related initiatives. The programming language JavaScript is flexible. Thanks to the release of technologies like Electron, developers working with JavaScript now have new possibilities. Using JavaScript, HTML, and CSS helps Electron build desktop apps compatible with several devices. Only two of the several well-known desktop programs created with Electron's help are Slack and Visual Studio Code. Using web technologies allows developers to create completely working desktop programs running without any problems across a spectrum of operating systems. This gives developers the ability to produce desktop apps.

Comparable to the above-mentioned method, JavaScript has also become clear as a good substitute in the field of game development. Though JavaScript has not always been connected with high-performance games, the development of WebGL and frameworks like Phaser has made it feasible to construct 2D and 3D games straight within the browser. This is so even if JavaScript is not usually associated with performance games. JavaScript can access the graphics hardware of a device by means of WebGL. This makes it possible to create visually rich games without depending on plugins or other software created by another company. The growth of web technologies that are getting more powerful and able to fit the standards of present gaming is making JavaScript a progressively important part of the game creation process.

Libraries like Johnny-Five are helping JavaScript get more and more involved in the Internet of Things related projects. Thanks to the availability of these libraries, developers may now create JavaScript code interacting with hardware parts. JavaScript has become a good substitute for the creation of Internet of Things applications needing functionality on the front-end and the back-end. The fact that JavaScript is becoming more easily available causes this. Using JavaScript on the device and the server allows developers to create consistent, scalable, easily maintainable full-stack Internet of Things systems. Developers may also be designing these solutions.

The growing importance of modern build tools and the technological ecology surrounding them is one of the most obvious aspects that has surfaced over the evolution of contemporary JavaScript. Developers can create code using the most contemporary ECMAScript features—including some not yet supported by all browsers—thanks in part to the JavaScript compiler called Babel. This enables creators of code to produce more effective versions. Your Babel is in charge of turning this current JavaScript into a version fit for previous iterations of the language. This guarantees, therefore, that apps may run on many different browsers and environments. The most efficient package management for JavaScript is currently generally agreed upon to be Node Package management, sometimes known as npm. This tool gives developers access to quickly manage dependencies, distribute libraries, and install packages produced by outside developers.

The introduction of these build tools and package managers has made it possible to create applications that are more modular, controlled, and efficient, therefore improving the process of development. These tools have become essential if we are to correctly control the complexity of contemporary web building. Given the great variety of JavaScript frameworks and libraries now accessible, this is especially true. Apart from this, they enable developers to automate repetitive tasks, therefore enhancing performance and simplifying the development process.

CONCLUSION

JavaScript is a dynamic, always changing universe that is essential to the modern digital experience; once you reach the conclusion of The Future of JavaScript - Coding Interactive Websites: A Beginner's Guide to JavaScript, you have taken your first significant trip into the realm of JavaScript. Activities like creating your first "Hello, World!" script and building interactive elements have helped you to develop your basic knowledge of the language running a major share of the internet today.

Along this journey, we have looked at JavaScript's grammar and structure as well as the reasoning for the interaction taking place on the web. You now possess the skills required to create responsive user experiences, dynamically modify content, manage events, validate forms, and interact with basic programming ideas such as loops, functions, arrays, and objects. The most crucial point is that you have personally seen how JavaScript can create dynamic and entertaining websites from still HTML pages.

Becoming a confident web developer requires theory to be put into action; you have achieved this by building an interactive project that is not just simple but also useful. Practicing hands-on coding helps you to start developing the attitude of problem-solving, which is absolutely important for working in real-world programming situations.

Our last section looked ahead at JavaScript and what it has in store for us. JavaScript's further growth outside its original intent has been facilitated by the deployment of ES6+ capabilities, the creation of robust frameworks like React and Vue, and the inclusion of technologies like Node.js and Progressive Web Apps. Originally a full-stack language, JavaScript has been developed to be used in running desktop software, mobile apps, and server-side systems. It spans more than just the browser now. The future of JavaScript is predicted to be more promising and flexible than it has ever been because of the explosion of artificial intelligence, real time apps, and even Internet of Things (IoT) development.

Maintaining your interest, coding, and learning are the most crucial things. Like with all other technologies, JavaScript's development will keep on. New tools will be created, best practices will be changed, and fresh elements will be introduced. Maintaining your skills and staying flexible in the face of whatever the future may bring will depend on keeping yourself actively committed and consistent in practice.

It was designed with the idea that everyone can learn to write and that JavaScript is among the most easily available and fulfilling approaches to get going. Now you have the tools, knowledge, and confidence required to begin shaping your own experiences on the internet, maybe one day you will be able to help the web itself to evolve.

I appreciate you joining us on this journey. Your career as a developer is in its second phase right now. Explore once more, keep building, and most importantly, keep enjoying the creative possibilities of code.

Thank you for buying and reading/ listening to our book. If you found this book useful/ helpful please take a few minutes and leave a review on the platform where you purchased our book. Your feedback matters greatly to us.

www.ingramcontent.com/pod-product-compliance
Lightning Source LLC
LaVergne TN
LVHW022102200926
848481LV00003B/1040
* 9 7 9 8 3 4 9 3 6 3 4 1 2 *